I love the name, Billie
My dad's was the same, Billie
I love the way they laugh and say
How silly to call that girl, Billie
Baffle them all, Billie
For at the call, Billie
They think it's so queer
That a girl should appear
Their illusions, I fear, I destroy
That is the reason my name's Billie
My parents expected a boy

From the Broadway stage production *Billie*, 1928.
Lyrics by George M. Cohan

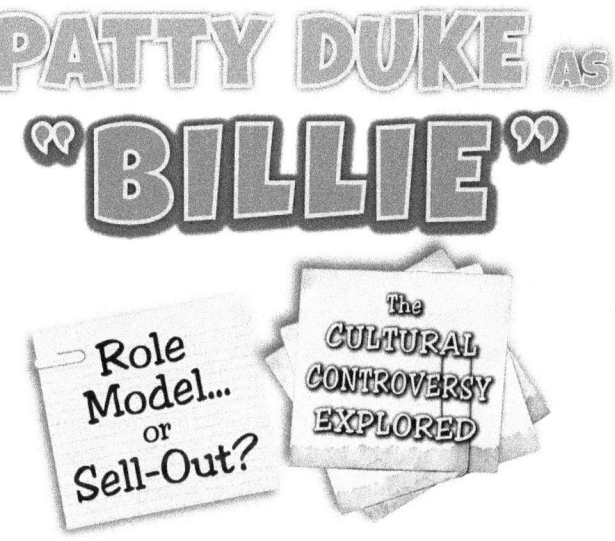

Gary Gerani and Casey Bond

Commentary by Patty Duke

Albany, Georgia

Patty Duke as Billie: Role Model or Sell-Out?

Copyright © 2015 Gary Gerani and Casey Bond. All Rights Reserved.

No part of this book may be reproduced in any form or by any means, electronic, mechanical, digital, photocopying or recording, except for the inclusion in a review, without permission in writing from the publisher.

Billie © 1965 Patricia Lawford Stewart and Anna Maria Pearce.

Published in the USA by
BearManor Media
P.O. Box 71426
Albany, GA 31708
www.BearManorMedia.com

ISBN: 1-59393-841-1

Library of Congress Control Number: 2015909889
BearManor Media, Albany, GA

Printed in the United States of America

PATTY DUKE AS "BILLIE"

Role Model... or Sell-Out?

The CULTURAL CONTROVERSY EXPLORED

Dedicated to Mark Patrick Carducci, the late, great writer from Bay Ridge, Brooklyn, who first introduced Gary Gerani to Casey Bond (Casey Cole at the time).

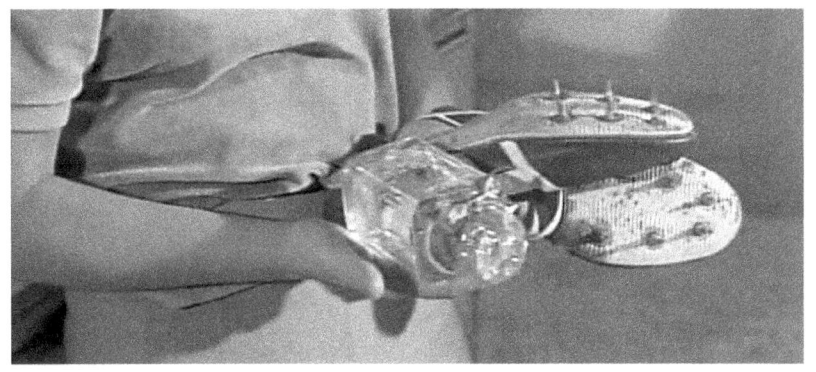

Table of Contents

Acknowledgments	xi
Introduction	xiii
A Chat with Anna	1
From Stage to Screen	7
The Making of "Billie"	25
The Story	35
Selling and Seeing "Billie"	127
The Controversy	135
The Beat Goes On	169
End Game: Some Final Thoughts	181
Additional Reading/Viewing	183
About the Authors	189

Acknowledgments

Our sincere thanks to:

Anna Pearce (Patty Duke) and husband Mike Pearce, who seemed to be having fun as we chatted about Billie, the way times have changed, and what beautiful wackos we human beings are.

Ben Ohmart, who surprised even me when he picked *Billie* from a dozen other book proposals I had shoved under his nose.

Bill Jankowski of the official Patty Duke Webpage, for hooking me up with Anna and Mike to begin with, and supporting this project in general.

Richard Kampmann, the accomplished California photographer who, as a high school kid, served as an extra on *Billie*. He was able to provide some invaluable first-hand recollections of the actual filming, along with great pictures of Duke in action… along with her Swedish stand-in.

Rock Baker, who deftly drew comic book character renderings of the new Billie.

Ken Rubin, project coordinator supreme, who helped me get all of the book's visuals safely to Ben through the modern miracle of DropBox.

The photographs used in this book come from the author's personal collection. They are either publicity photos issued by United Artists, newswire images, or candid shots. In a few cases, such as the "perfume or sneakers?" picture on the Contents page, a frame grab from the movie was used.

Introduction

A BOOK ABOUT *BILLIE*? THAT SILLY TOMBOY MOVIE WITH PATTY DUKE in a tracksuit? Are you serious?

This was generally the first reaction to what is clearly an unexpected subject for scholarly analysis. Even Miss Duke herself couldn't resist giggling at first. Why spend time and energy exploring the virtues of a mostly forgotten family film from the 1960s, a seemingly light-hearted rites of passage comedy that Patty filmed toward the end of her teen-themed TV series, and just before her wickedly perverse 'grown-up' turn in *Valley of the Dolls*?

Why indeed.

To answer this, let's travel back in time to that age of relative innocence, the late '70s, as we join young Gary Gerani and Casey Bond in their rented Lefrak apartment in Sheepshead Bay, Brooklyn. It happens to be 'Women's Lib' week on *The 4:30 Movie*, and as Gerani returns from a hard day at the Topps Chewing Gum office, he happens to catch the film's finale, as does his companion/roommate Casey. They watch super-sportsgirl Billie in what amounts to a pink prom dress, happily dumping her athletic ambitions and potential Olympics immortality for the bliss of first romance with Warren Berlinger. "Just to be glad I'm a girl is my greatest victory," the former tomboy/ace runner warbles in her closing musical number.

The ensuing discussion between Casey Bond and myself didn't last very long, but we managed to overview the key issues of this social debate with a minimum of personal ire. Happily, it wasn't one of our more vitriolic marathon exchanges.

But it was damned interesting, even enjoyable, reflecting our own journey as youngsters in the tumultuous '60s, which very much influenced our views as young adults in the 1970s. Like so many of us Boomers, I watched Patty Duke grow up on the big and small screen, first as handicapped Helen Keller in *The Miracle Worker*, then as identical cousins with delightfully opposite personalities on her popular ABC-TV series. I remember seeing *Billie* as a kid and responding to Patty in her relatively sexy shorty-shorts with typical male adolescent fascination – suddenly everybody's favorite surrogate sister was growing up, looking awfully cute in Technicolor. I was also vaguely familiar with Ronald Alexander's play *Time Out for Ginger*, which had been fully accepted by critics and audiences as *the* 'tomboy finds romance' story of post-war America, something of an answer to *Little Women*. Bouncing around United Artists for a few years (ZIV even did a TV pilot in 1960 – read all about it in the next chapter!), *Ginger* seemed like the ideal vehicle for seventeen year-old Patty Duke as she transitioned from child star to full-fledged adult actress. So Duke made the movie, an inexpensive semi-musical, it played theatrically with little fanfare before winding up on television, and that was pretty much that. Or so it seemed.

Flash forward to the grumpy 21st Century. By accident, I happen to stumble upon *Billie* as listed in the IMDb, and I'm amazed to see the very same argument of tomboy vs. girly-girl being played out in the film's reader reaction posts. Most people who remembered *Billie* from their childhood waxed nostalgia about go-go dancing and the Gidget-like pleasures of

INTRODUCTION

a simpler time, just before Viet Nam exploded. Some praised the movie's stance on equal rights for athletic girls and pooh-poohed the 'sell-out' ending, citing conventions of the day. Besides, Rosalind Russell usually gave up her man's world profession for a loving hubby in the final act of her classic movies, yet she's still generally hailed as a proto-feminist and an inspiration for independent-minded women. Why should Patty Duke's rebellious femme ("I want to be treated as an equal first, a girl second!") be viewed any differently? As might be expected, most younger responders, raised to take gender equality for granted, were horrified by the heroine's decision to trade her remarkable uniqueness for girly-girl rewards. What kind of message is this sending, they perhaps rightfully asked?

2626 Homecrest Avenue, in Sheepshead Bay, Brooklyn, New York. Our apartment was second from the top, far right side of the building. This neighborhood, famed for its seafood restaurants, hasn't really changed all that much since the 1970s.

Intrigued by these political and social reactions to *Billie*, I decided to put the whole discussion between two covers and bring my wonderful lover and debating partner back into the mix... our chat was indeed ground zero for the great *Billie* Controversy, so this return was fitting. We again watched the movie together – this time in glorious CinemaScope – and had a grand old time traveling back to the past, savoring all attendant, non-cynical Greatest Generation comforts. And then we started talking about individual choice/personal freedom vs. an obligation to social progress... and the fascinating subtext of *Billie* surfaced again. Playwright Ronald Alexander may have been churning out yet another comical *Father Knows Best* scenario in the 1950s, a precursor to family-themed TV sitcoms, but the heartfelt angst and progressive agenda of Ginger/Billie continues to resonate, perhaps more strongly now than ever before.

Adding fuel to this intellectual fire was yet another consideration: is the Billie character gay? Are we dealing with some kind of gender disorder, or perhaps merely a girl's now acceptable right to behave and dress like a boy if she wants to? Is a sex-change operation a viable option for Billie, or are we simply overreacting to a traditionally heterosexual, 'awkward age' rites of passage interlude? Despite the stereotype, not all tomboys are gay; many resent that classification. The fact that Billie's iconic hoyden hairstyle resembles Ellen Degeneres' boyish 'do only complicates matters.

So here we are, facing a book of unexpected questions and some cool pictures of Billie doing her thing. What could be more endearing than America's girl-next-door sweetheart, Patty Duke, running races with the Shaggy Dog, standing up to Mel Cooley on the subject of women's rights, and singing her angst-ridden little heart out about being a "lonely little in-between"? For the pure joy of pop nostalgia, spiced so intriguingly with pertinent social issues that are brimming just below the surface, there's hardly a better subject for exploration than this 1965 United Artists release.

A book about *Billie*... silly? Not for those of us who realize what Ronald Alexander was sneaking into his otherwise innocuous confection. As the titular heroine herself points out, people who are passive rather than active are ultimately cowards. Please consider *Patty Duke as Billie: Role Model or Sell-Out?* an act of personal courage on my part. Renewing an old debate with super-thinker Casey Bond took guts, believe me… but the irresistible subject matter and resulting intellectual rewards brought smiles to our faces. Join both of us now, Baby Boomers entering Phase Three of life's surprising journey, as we lace up our sneakers and beat a path toward the truth…

A Chat with Anna

On January 11, 2013, I had the pleasure of interviewing Patty Duke, known to most these days as Anna Pearce, on the subject of *Billie*. Along the way, we discussed the difficulty of being an 'in-between', the social and political changes since the mid-1960s, and the challenges all Billie-age youngsters face in the comparatively brittle 21st Century.

On this project: "I think it's so fabulous that you're doing a book on *Billie*. I couldn't get any interviews when we made the movie."

On Billie's rebellion: "She wasn't very enlightened, but this was forty years ago (pre-feminist era). She did stand up for her beliefs, and knew enough about her constitutional rights. She wasn't restricted by her family. She had the courage to defy authority, unlike me at the time. I just did what I was told.

I never knew why I had to have yellow hair as Billie, for example. I never balked about it. I had no mind of my own. Until 18."

On homosexuality: "I'm of the opinion that people don't choose to be gay; they're born with that. To be able to look at a movie like *Billie* that's non-threatening, but touches some of the emotions these kids have, which they can't show because they're supposed to be so sophisticated... and angry. That's of real value. I didn't think I was playing a gay character when I did it. I just pulled from my own feelings. *Billie* in a way was paralleling my life at the time. But what I was going through, the anguish of feeling like an outsider, happened to be exactly what a lot of homosexual kids were feeling. That's one of the reasons *Billie* has a huge gay following."

On "Butterflies" and showbiz slavery: "I don't know that I realized it at the time, but the picture had that song about "Butterflies..." I knew that feeling, I knew what it was like to have one foot in freedom, and one foot in slavery. I did recognize that, and I did use it (in my performance). It was very inspirational. Of all the songs I've sung, or tried to sing, "Funny Little Butterflies" was probably the closest to who I really am. Remember, I was not allowed to be a teenager, not a normal teenager. I had a princess phone... but it was never connected! Can you believe that? Kids in show business are little slaves."

On her dramatic performance in Billie: "I think it works. The little girl, or young teenager... you believed that she really felt what she was talking about, and singing about. I think the portrayal is real."

On her physical performance in Billie: "Ha! The whole thing was a sham. I've never been terribly athletic. I had so many doubles on *Billie*! I may have done two hurdles after practicing endlessly. To coach me they called in (Olympics champion) Rafer Johnson, who was the real deal. He was hired mainly for publicity reasons. I had a double for all the dancing, too. Donna (McKechnie, later famed for *A Chorus Line*) taught me a few steps, but I was a joke, really. That was the one thing I didn't like about making *Billie* – I wanted to do everything myself. Except pole vault."

On her gender-bending alter-ego: "They needed someone to double for me, which wasn't easy, because I'm short. So they came back with a boy who was a junior in that high school. And the next thing I knew, he had on the shorts, and the hair, and the boobs – not much to brag about, but something – and he got the job done. Then the kid went back to his school right after that, and his life became miserable… all the ribbing he took for doubling a girl!"

On coloring her hair blonde: "I hated it! I would have to get my hair bleached twice a week… This led to really painful sores on my scalp. On *The Patty Duke Show*, I had a Patty Wig and a Cathy wig, that was that. But on *Billie*, they were too cheap to get me one! And the shooting time was short. So they put me through that ordeal."

On working with director Don Weis (veteran of TPDS): "He made me laugh, every day. He smoked cigars and had the energy of about twelve people. In many ways Don was a cheerleader for me, which I always appreciated. In terms of dramatic preparation, I got 'deep' into the character myself, finding Billie's feelings through my own inner (explorations), rather than from specific advice (from the director). We were on a very tight schedule… which is why I didn't have a wig! But (Don Weis) didn't talk down to me… he treated me as an equal. He was the perfect choice for me, and that movie in particular…

On a couple of hunky co-stars: "If I wasn't so busy trying to do the part, I would have fallen in love with Warren Berlinger (Billie's first boyfriend, Mike Benson). Part of me did. And he was much older than me, but I just thought he was the bee's knees. And Bobby Diamond (Billie's sexist rival Eddie Davis)… he was so sweet. And I couldn't figure out how he could be so mean (on screen). He was one of those really nice, get-along kind of guys. The rest of the cast was wonderful, too. No problems at all. *Billie* was one of the few times I really had fun making a movie."

On movie musical scoring: "Music really stirs our soul… and so if it's used properly in a film, it can evoke emotions that may not be coming otherwise. When someone sings a song, they portray every human element…"

On the difference between movie and theater performing: "When you do film, you depend on the director to be your audience. When you do a play, that's multiplied by however many seats are filled before you. It's an extraordinary sense of acceptance, and love. For me, you can't beat it."

On the film's financial performance: "They were sure it was going to be a really big hit… but it barely made any box office money. It cost very little to make, of course. And, as we can see, it's become something of a cult film."

On the film and character's lasting impact: "When you think about it, it's an early *Rocky*. Not nearly as good, but kind of valid. I even think you can bring *Billie* back. So many teenagers are unhappy these days… I wouldn't want to be growing up now.

If *Billie* were to be brought back, I think it should be done as realistically as possible. It should be about people who are 'in-betweens'. When the movie first came out… I loved it. I loved what I saw. I was thankful for my performance. And as the years have gone on, I love it even more. It's what we've been talking about, about what movies do for us… what they rekindle in us. And for me, it was helping me make my personal transition, from little girl to young adult woman. But I also love it because I was so *game*. Ha! They said you're gonna have to run, and pole vault, and jump the hurdles… And, I thought, 'wait till they see me!'

Finally, on our ultimate thematic question: *Is Billie Carol a role model or a sell-out for giving up athletic ambitions in favor of first romance?* Anna's answer... will not be revealed at this time. First, let's take this pop-social journey ourselves, exploring with an open mind the history, reception and enduring legacy of all things *Billie*.

Patty Duke, better known as Anna Pearce, in 2012.

From Stage to Screen

BILLIE BEGAN LIFE AS RONALD ALEXANDER'S PLAY *TIME OUT FOR GINGER*, which ran for 248 performances at the Lyceum Theatre on Broadway from November 26, 1952 to June 27, 1953. Set almost entirely in a middle class family's living room, *Ginger* was a happy success for all concerned, not only in New York, but in regional theaters throughout the country. Hollywood's Melvyn Douglas played befuddled small town banker Howard Carol in both the Broadway production and a Chicago incarnation, the latter offering promising newcomer Steve McQueen as a teen hothead. Nancy Malone, a New York actress who later portrayed police detective Paul Burke's wife in *Naked City* (ABC TV), debuted in the feisty title role.

Ginger's airy plotline (according to the Herald Tribune's overview) concerns a banker who requires "some kind of creative release and finds it by lecturing to local high school classes on the need for self-fulfillment. It quickly develops however, that one of his daughters – the youngest of three –

has been very much impressed by her father's exhortations. She has further decided that her own true fulfillment can best be realized by going out for the football team." Predictably, this decision leads to all kinds of calamitous/humorous complications: the banker's job is jeopardized by a grousing, old-fashioned president; the girl's teenage sisters resent what's happening to their social life; and the football player herself has trouble reconciling athletic ambitions with her boyfriend's reflexive disapproval. Domestic hi-jinks inevitably ensue, but everything ends agreeably as a plethora of conflicts are resolved, foremost among them the young quarterback's decision to trade pigskin victories for more traditional, 'ladylike' romantic experiences. Loving feelings are reassured all around and *Ginger* concludes breezily with the entire family heading out to see one of the older daughters performing in a local play.

Family-friendly comedies were commonplace on Broadway in the post-war era, and critics had mostly glowing things to say about Alexander's good-natured romp. "Another highly enjoyable comedy has come to town," declared the N.Y. Times. "The theme of the tomboy who finds herself ditched by her boyfriend for conduct unbecoming a girl leads to some tender moments at the end. And a comedy that not only amuses but moves an audience is irresistible." The World Telegram was equally enthusiastic: "*Time Out for Ginger* is hilarious, all right, but it is also human, warm and touching. Draws as steady a stream of laughs as any comedy in years."

Significantly, none of these reviews address the controversial social implications of Ginger's athletic prowess and goals… the very elements that differentiate *Time Out* from similar family confections. The reliable trope of a tomboy 'growing up', abandoning sports and embracing her femininity (usually punctuated by said female's climactic appearance in a dress by tale's end) had been so accepted as a charmingly bittersweet rite of passage that even the most progressive critics were oblivious to what was bubbling just below the surface.

From Stage to Screen

Nancy Malone was the first actress to tackle the role of Ginger (aka Billie) Carol. Insert: That's a young Steve McQueen as Eddie Davis, about to get popped.

Interestingly, there are indications throughout the play that author Ronald Alexander is in truth a pre-feminist, or at the least an open-minded pragmatist. Far more significant than the latest *Life with Father*-style shenanigans is the genuine sense of outrage felt by sports-craving Ginger Carol and the ensuing, frustrating war with local 'reactionaries' that she wages. Her rebellious stance anticipates the more front-and-center social upheavals of a decade later. Keeping conservative '50s attitudes in mind, let's consider some key dialogue exchanges that reflect this emerging attitude:

Howard Carol has made some unfortunate public remarks about high school athletics for females. Now at home after a hard day, he faces a few bracing questions from ever-sensible wife Agnes and two of his three daughters.

Howard: Well, I didn't mean to abolish gym for girls. Basically it was a speech on manners.

Joan: You mean you approve of gym for girls?

Howard: Well, not exactly…

He removes his suddenly controversial speech from a breast pocket and starts reading aloud.

Howard: I said, "perhaps one reason that young men do not conform to the rules of etiquette is that they see girls playing volleyball and basketball, thus losing sight of their femininity."

Joan: And then you said it.

Howard: Yeah. Huh? Well, extemporaneously I may have said that perhaps one idea might be to change the method of gym for girls.

Agnes: What sort of change, dear?

Howard: Instead of rough sports let them take long walks during those periods.

Jeannie (*face lighting up*)**:** I agree with you, Daddy.

Joan (*equally pleased*)**:** So do I.

Howard (*breathing a sigh of relief*)**:** It stands to reason, Agnes, that competitive sports are too violent for young girls.

Patty Duke as "Billie"

Top: Hollywood veteran Melvyn Douglas as loving dad Howard Carol. Bottom: Chester Morris played Howard and Liza Minnelli was Ginger in a 1964 Bucks County Playhouse, Pennsylvania revival.

Agnes: I'll bet the school board is looking for the highest tree in town right now.

Jeannie: I think Daddy absolutely put his finger on the root of the problem.

Joan: I think your speech was positively breathtaking.

Just then, Ginger blows into the house, clearly ticked-off about something.

Ginger: I think all men stink.

Howard: Don't retract that remark just because I'm here.

Ginger: I wasn't going to.

Agnes: What's wrong between you and Tommy today?

Ginger: He always wants me to do something I don't want to do, because he doesn't want me to do something he doesn't want me to do. That's the trouble with men.

Jeannie: What does Tommy want you to do?

Ginger: Be a cheerleader.

Later, Joan's annoying jock boyfriend Eddie Davis shows up at the Carol home. He and Ginger appear to be frequent sparring partners.

Ginger: Hiya, musclehead.

Eddie: Hiya, kid.

Ginger (*to her parents and sisters*): He insulted me.

Eddie: I did not!

Ginger: You did so, you reactionary. He called Tommy Green a sissy.

Howard: I don't see how that concerns you.

Ginger: Every time one boy wants to insult another, he calls him a sissy. And by that they imply that girls are inferior to boys. So yesterday after school, when the track team was out I challenged him to a hundred yard dash.

Eddie: I didn't want to race a girl.

Ginger: At first he just laughed, but after I needled him for a while, he said he'd show me.

Howard: Well, what happened?

Ginger (*looking at Eddie*): I ran him into the ground.

Agnes: You mean you beat him.

Ginger: By five yards.

Eddie (*indignant*): *Three* yards!

Howard laughs.

Things get a little more serious when the school principal shows up and demands that Virginia abandon her athletic ambitions at Harding. Even Agnes is accused of being 'old-fashioned' ("You've accepted the theory that women shouldn't compete with men," snarls Ginger) as the unexpected equal rights debate rages on.

Howard: Virginia, if you persist in this nonsense, I'll cut off your allowance.

Ginger: I don't need any money, I'm in training. You see, Pop, I don't ask to be on the team. All I ask is a chance to try out for it.

Agnes: But, darling, I don't think you're equipped to play football.

Ginger: You can't say that until you've given me a chance.

Agnes: But you're a girl.

Ginger: Lots of athletes are.

Howard: They don't play football against men.

Ginger: *Because men won't let them.* You're supposed to be sports, and all the time you're afraid we'll be equal to you.

Agnes: Or better than you...

Another socially-charged conversation occurs between voice-of-reason Agnes and her petulant, non-athletic daughters. Much to Joan's dismay, sibling Jeannie cheerfully arcs from self-obsessed ninny to progressive activist.

Joan: We don't believe a girl should be allowed to play football.

Jeannie: It's just not right, Mother.

Agnes: In other words, anything you disagree with is wrong and should be stopped. Is that it?

Jeannie: Well, we feel Ginger should be allowed to do whatever she wants to do, as long as it's not playing football.

Joan: That's the resolution passed by the girls of the senior and junior classes.

Agnes: By majority vote?

Jeannie: Of course, Mother.

Agnes: I see. By democratic procedure, you have both decided to tear up the Bill of Rights. That's very interesting. If you hadn't, you'd defend Virginia's right to play whether you agreed with it or not. You know you could both take a very good lesson from your father. He stands to lose his job, but he'd rather take that chance than deprive your sister of her freedom of choice.

Jeannie (*genuinely inspired*): Gee! Daddy is a kind of Joan of Arc character. Well, from now on, I'm going to the games.

Joan is horrified by Jeannie's turncoat behavior, branding her sister "a traitor to American womanhood, per se." But the suddenly enlightened teenager's on a roll.

Jeannie: I'm going over to Ginger's side, and if Eddie Davis makes one more remark about her or Dad, I'll kick him all over the school!

Here's an interesting Agnes-Ginger exchange that nails some arguably unintentional sexist condescension from the football players on Ginger's team. Harding High does indeed win the much-anticipated big game, and distaff player Ginger, a novelty, scores as their star performer... but has this young athlete really been given an honest opportunity to demonstrate her considerable skills? Bummed out Ginger explains it all to Mom:

Ginger: Well, the last few seconds of the game the boys called time out. They wanted me to play, so they told Eddie to walk off quietly or they'd throw him off bodily. They knew the other team had to punt. The kicker went back to his end zone. Our line crashed through. He had to rush the kick. It was a bad punt that wobbled down to the twenty. They let me take it, then opened a hole in the center that a slow freight could have gone through. They were determined I'd score.

Agnes: Well, isn't that the purpose of the game?

Ginger: But, Mom, they all treated me like something special, not just like anybody carrying the mail.

Agnes: What about those three men who had you trapped?

Ginger: When I got to them, I slowed up. By that time I didn't want the touchdown. I wanted them to tackle me.

Agnes: And they didn't?

Ginger: They were laughing so hard, they fell flat on their faces. I *had* to score.

Agnes: But didn't that touchdown win the game?

Ginger: Mom… by the time I got into the game we were leading thirty-four to nothing! (*When it was over*) they picked me up on their shoulders, like a curio, and marched me around the field. Both teams. With Daddy leading them. I was furious. I kept shouting, "Put me down! Put me down!"

Ironically, the girl athlete's embarrassing victory parade is eventually revisited in Billie, *but in a different context: no one 'allows' Billie to win Harding's decathlon; she overwhelms the boys decisively with her built-in Beat. But Carol's still treated like 'a curio', and appears confused and deflated as she's paraded about, weeping enigmatically, by her macho teammates.*

Time Out for Ginger's success in theatrical venues across the country eventually led to television, a fledgling medium ideally suited to family comedies with heart. On October 6, 1955, an hour-long production of Alexander's play, directed by Ralph Levy, was broadcast on CBS' prestigious *Shower of Stars* anthology series. Playing Howard Carol was none other than Jack Benny, somehow transcending his famous persona and giving Harding's daughter-ridden banker/frustrated quarterback his due. Others in the lively cast included Ruth Hussey as Agnes, Gary Crosby as Eddie Davis, Edward Everett Horton as Ed Hoffman, Mary Wickes as Lizzie the maid, Larry Keating as W.J. Archer, John Hoyt as Principal Wilson, Ronnie Burns as Tommy Green, Olive Sturgess as Mia Carroll (renamed from Jeannie),

Carol Leigh as Joan Carroll, and a spirited young actress named Janet Parker as Ginger. Most of the play's original scenes remain in this truncated but faithful adaptation (which required three writers), although Agnes' relatively daring "you're tearing up the Bill of Rights" speech to her daughters was cut, probably for practical reasons. It's one of the play's few major scenes without Howard in it, or in this case, superstar Jack Benny. Fortunately, he is present for Ginger's most damning declarations, which include nailing the men in her life for only pretending to be good sports, when in reality they're afraid of being bested by the 'weaker' sex.

Toward decade's end, ZIV (later United Artists Television), noting the success of TV shows like *Leave it to Beaver* and *Dennis the Menace*, prepared a genuine half-hour pilot based on *Time Out for Ginger*. Gambling that a distaff version of the 'terrible tyke' formula might fly in 1960, producer Lewis J. Rachmil went directly to the source and hired Ronald Alexander to rethink his *Ginger* premise for a weekly series.

Several key characters gain insight during the course of the original play, discovering through romantic misadventure and comical mishap the error of limited thinking. Obviously this kind of life-changing epiphany needed to be slowed-down, divided into an ongoing series of mini-lessons, learned one episode at a time. Alexander eliminated Howard Carol's foot-in-mouth puritanism and re-imagined him as something more palatable for a sitcom: the flustered but wise, ever-patient patriarch. This latest incarnation (played by veteran film/radio actor Karl Swenson) doesn't make dumb speeches about women's rights; he's too busy shooting rockets into space as a research physicist at Cape Canaveral. Surrounded by females (one wife, two daughters, and a wisecracking maid), Dr. Carol's only real dilemma is surviving the amped-up antics of his adoring thirteen year-old daughter. As noted by a few industry critics, indefatigable Ginger is essentially playing Dennis to Howard's more dignified version of 'good old Mr. Wilson.'

She's just an angel in jeans in her terrible teens
She's a gal all her pals call Ginger.
She's fun… She'll run…
And laugh at the slightest notion
She'll dream… Then beam…
Look out for the big explosion!

As the theme song suggests, Ginger, portrayed full-out by ponytailed Candy Moore, explodes with tomboyish enthusiasm at the drop of a baseball cap. Her borderline surreal, super-spunky persona suggests a hyperactive child in desperate need of medication, a far cry from the play's angst-ridden athlete rightfully outraged by sexist rules and restrictions. One can only surmise that Alexander's decision to change his male protagonist from banker to Werner von Braun was to create an easy, breezy metaphor: precocious Ginger is akin to one of Dr. Carol's supersonic missiles, the unbridled result of progressive parenting. Will this experiment work, or has the good doctor created a monster? According to wife Agnes (Maggie Hayes) and maid

Lizzie (Margaret Hamilton, sans broomstick), their resident force of nature gets herself into the craziest of jams at least partially because Daddy's such a pushover. He's also something of a human punching bag, often on the receiving end of his exuberant daughter's loving elbow jabs.

Rounding out ZIV's proposed version of the Carol clan is older teenage daughter Joan, played by Roberta Shore, who'd achieve small screen fame a few years later on *The Virginian* series. Extra sibling Jeannie (renamed 'Mia' on *Shower of Stars*) was eliminated for expediency, and this cleaner 'double daughter' arrangement – one a tomboy, the other a girly-girl – would be retained by Alexander for his *Billie* screenplay. Another major character reworked from the play was Joan's jock boyfriend Eddie Davis (John Rockwell), presented here as the ideal foil for his girlfriend's fun-craving sister. Ginger's too young in this incarnation to believably out-perform Davis athletically; instead, she gleefully drives him nuts with an endless barrage of playful put-downs.

The plot chosen for ZIV's pilot establishes a simple formula that makes logical use of all regular players. Joan's need of a vehicle for a very important date soon takes center stage, prompting boisterous, overconfident Ginger to promise her sister wheels. Unfortunately, Howard's using the family car on the night in question, forcing his little 'angel in jeans' into emergency mode. With spunk to spare and a million dollar smile, Ginger's all about town and going for broke, using every precocious trick in the book to secure a car for Jean's all-important night out. These comical scenes with supporting characters and guest stars provide a pretty clear picture of Moore's terrible/adorable tomboy in action, giving viewers a good idea of what to expect in future installments.

It seems despondent Ginger has failed to achieve her goal when sympathetic Howard, who was slyly testing his daughter in order to teach her a lesson about responsibility, offers her the family car. Much to his surprise and delight, Ginger turns down the offer... it was her goofy mistake, she reasons, she'll have to live with the consequences. This from a loud thirteen-year-old who generally acts like she's eight. In the only exchange lifted intact from Alexander's stage script, daughter and father enjoy some wistful words about their very special bond, now and in future years ("Can I always tell you my secrets, Daddy?"). It's a curious development. After spending most of the episode getting irritated by this head-in-the-clouds scientist Dad and his obnoxious loud-mouthed offspring, viewers are finally allowed to share an honest, intimate moment with them, and it works. Fittingly, Ginger's unexpected maturity under fire winds up earning her a storybook-style reward at tale's end, as all of the outside parties she approached show up to help.

So that's the concept, TV execs: Every week viewers laugh themselves silly as childlike misfit Ginger Carol propels herself into ever-escalating teenage jams. But by using her wits – she's a rocket scientist's daughter, after all – and following her heart, Ginger always manages to beat the odds and save the day, earning a prideful smile from the long-suffering man in her life, Dad. There's your series.

Pre-teen Candy Moore, star of Tomboy and the Champ *and soon-to-be regular on* The Lucy Show, *played a boisterous Ginger, opposite Karl Swenson as her overwhelmed dad.*

Or not. Whether it was a case of Ginger being too hyper or the idea of a female Dennis the Menace rubbing some old schoolers the wrong way, all three networks and major syndicators passed. TV somehow missed its golden-age teenage tomboy series, despite how perfectly suited the genre was to a small screen, week-to-week incarnation. 1965's *Gidget* revisited the formula with some success, offering Sally Field and Don Porter in a similar daughter-father vein, although Francie Lawrence's jams had as much in common with older sister Joan's romantic dilemmas as they did with Ginger's rambunctious ones.

Also making significant pop-TV waves in the early 1960s was a little sitcom known as *The Patty Duke Show*. After winning a well-deserved Oscar for playing famously handicapped Helen Keller in *The Miracle Worker*, a role she originated on Broadway, Patty Duke defied child star expectations the way equally offbeat/supremely gifted Jodie Foster would in the 1970s. A harmless family series for ABC-TV seemed reasonable at this juncture of her career, and *TPDS* wound up earning her a huge, devoted fan base that persists to this day. Portraying twin cousins Patty and Cathy Lane in a show packaged by Peter Lawford's production company, Chrislaw, Miss Duke scored as a sympathetic everygirl: spirited, appealing, abstractly funny a la Lucy when required, yet somehow real and imperfect, not a cutie pie in the expected Sandra Dee or Debbie Reynolds mold. The unique demands of Duke's double role reminded everyone that this was indeed a legitimate Oscar-winning actress delivering some nuanced work... serving up bubble gum Americana no question, but with a little textured reality about the edges.

Lasting a solid three seasons, *The Patty Duke Show* became a reliable, efficiently-made (given all the split-screen work), well-licensed property for United Artists Television, formerly ZIV... yes, by coincidence, the very same company that tried to launch *Time Out for Ginger* a few years earlier. Now events were about to elevate Ronald Alexander's awkward but durable brainchild into a new, relatively spectacular configuration, with all creative elements, legal rights, and various career needs neatly dovetailing into place.

This page: Patty Duke as Helen Keller and Anne Bancroft as Annie Sullivan in 1962's The Miracle Worker, *which earned Duke both an Oscar and a popular weekly television series on ABC,* The Patty Duke Show *(opposite page).*

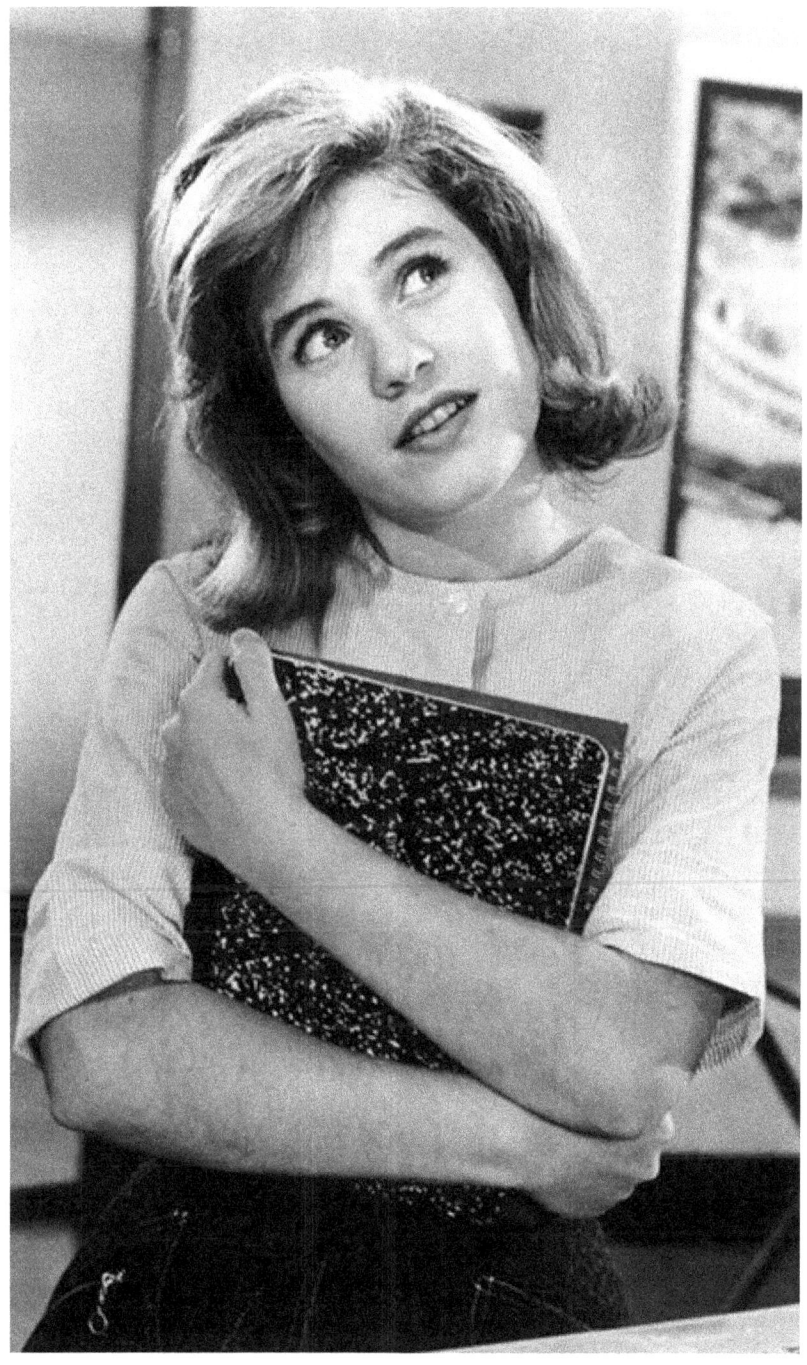

Together again: Anne Bancroft visits her Miracle Worker *co-star, Patty Duke, on the set of* Billie.

The Making of "Billie"

It isn't clear who suggested the *Ginger* property to actor/producer Peter Lawford and Patty Duke's career managers, but it was still attached to United Artists, as was Chrislaw's *The Patty Duke Show*. A new movie could be cross-promoted on the series every week. UA even managed to work a pre-deal with NBC for a future television showing that practically paid for the entire enterprise.

Playing a tomboy on the verge of first romance wouldn't exactly be a stretch for top-billed Duke, but getting into shape for the role's physical demands proved more than a little intimidating. Hired as her well-publicized technical advisor was no one less than 1960 Olympics legend Rafer Johnson. Track running, high-jumping, pole-vaulting and shot putting were among the ten decathlon exercises that would be depicted in the film, with Duke giving each and every one her personal best.

But the most significant creative alteration was yet to come. To differentiate itself from Chrislaw's vaguely similar TV series and reflecting mid-'60s pop taste in general, Alexander's venerable storyline would be reworked for modest but spirited teen-themed production numbers. In other words, after two cheap TV productions and countless stage incarnations, *Time Out for Ginger* was actually becoming a Hollywood musical... and from the releasing company that gave the world *West Side Story*, no less.

In truth, this idea wasn't as strange as it may have initially seemed. Duke, already a successful teen recording artist, would warble a few heartfelt songs that couldn't help but become hits, and did. She and co-star Warren Berlinger knew they'd be doubled in a spry dance number set in Harding High's auditorium, prancing out of close-up (often out-of-frame altogether) whenever more demanding moves were required. Choreographers from both *Shindig* and *Hullabaloo*, TV's reigning teen music series, were recruited by Chrislaw to devise spirited numbers to be performed on the high school playing field, in the locker room, the auditorium stage, and a local club. Among various accomplished dancers out for some kicks: a few former Jets from *West Side Story*, and a pre-*Chorus Line*'s Donna McKechnie, who receives both an opening title credit as *Billie*'s co-choreographer and a big close-up in the auditorium number. She reported to director/mentor Michael Bennett and David Winters, the latter famous for coordinating colorful dance routines for numerous Elvis and *Beach Party* movies.

Named as director of this agreeable oddity was Don Weis, veteran of nine *TPDS* episodes and very much appreciated for his efficient, budget-conscious methods. Chrislaw's idea was to shoot quickly – *very* quickly, 15 days – while the TV series was on hiatus. Weis had considerable experience with teenage musical romps, having cut his professional teeth over at MGM in the early '50s with frothy Debbie Reynolds vehicles like *I Love Melvin* and *The Affairs of Dobie Gillis* (not to mention more recent, less resume-worthy AIP confections like *Pajama Party* and *Ghost in the Invisible Bikini*). *Time Out for Ginger* was almost like coming home for this veteran director, a return to the kind of inoffensive family fare Hollywood dished out regularly during its celebrated golden age.

By design, this new United Artists movie was directly aimed at the same young audience that made *TPDS* a sustained hit. Since Patty's fans had no trouble accepting their idol as the diametrically different Lane cousins, a third, entirely different look and persona seemed to somehow continue this winning formula. Duke's page boy haircut, strikingly blonde and wig-like (it wasn't), would help her establish a convincing on-screen identity apart from the popular TV characterizations that pretty much set this project in motion.

And then there was the title.

For the first time in its creative history, *Time Out for Ginger* would be called something other than what its author intended. Nobody remembers why Ginger ultimately became Billie, although this new moniker subtly suggests boyishness rather than sauciness, perhaps a more accurate reflection of Duke's mostly low-key rebel. It's also possible that someone remembered the ancient George M. Cohan musical *Billie*, another feel-good Broadway show about an unconventional girl with a boy's name. A third theory points to the popular 1960s television series *Gilligan's Island*, which featured a prominent Ginger of its own (Tina Louise), not to mention future *Billie* dad Jim Backus. Regardless of name, Weis' sporty heroine had arrived and America's sweetheart Patty Duke was playing her. Now all that remained was to shoot the damn movie.

Ronald Alexander was once again called upon to re-work his play for a different creative venue. *Billie*'s musical numbers, while busy, were relatively limited and happily unobtrusive. The 87-minute movie format allowed for a structure similar to the original play, enabling Alexander to focus and tighten his thematic material. Gimmicks like the rocket scientist dad were out, although a new one, Billie's internal 'Beat' that propels her to fantastic athletic heights, was added. Football playing was changed to less abusive running/ decathlon sports. Social and political elements were made stronger and linked more believably with a better developed story and warmer characterizations. Most importantly, Duke's star status demanded that it clearly be Billie's movie, rather than her colorful father's, as in all previous adaptations. She is the first cast member we meet as this growing pains parable begins, and the last one we see as the end titles roll. And with an actress of PD's inherent skill and sensitivity essaying the part, Billie would be presented as an offbeat, slightly unexpected combination of cartoon-like caricature, at least visually, and legitimate angst-ridden teenager whose recognizable secret pain might take the casual viewer by surprise. It would turn out to be the perfect transitional role for teenager Patty Duke, reminding viewers that this pint-sized Oscar winner could bring memorable dramatic weight and remarkable craft to even the most unassuming of projects.

Chrislaw backed up their winsome star with a veritable who's who of sitcom personalities, all of them beloved character actors who audiences of the day never seemed to tire of. In one little movie we're treated to Jim Backus (*Gilligan's Island*), Dick Sargent (Darrin II from *Bewitched*), Richard Deacon (*The Dick Van Dyke Show*), Ted Bessell (Don Hollinger from *That Girl*), along with the larger-than-like antics of irascible Billy Dee Wolfe and Charles Lane.

In deliberate contrast to these funny guys is wry, dry Agnes Carol, the perfect Mom/voice of reason played with gentle irony by former noir star Jane Greer, still amazingly beautiful twenty years after her heyday. Even Billie's omnipresent English sheep dog Clown was enacted by a star, the same energetic pooch who charmed kiddies in Disney's *The Shaggy Dog* a few years earlier.

Shooting was limited to a few appropriate locations, among them John Marshall High School in Los Feliz, CA (immortalized years later as Rydell in *Grease*). But for most of the decathlon scenes, cast and crew descended upon University High in West L.A. Dave Wyman, now an award-winning pro photographer, was part of the school track team back in 1965. Along with many of his teammates, he was happily employed as an extra on *Billie*, and in 2006 he recalled some interesting aspects of the movie's production:

"The shoot, which lasted parts of three days, was a lot of fun. I have no idea how it happened, but the film employed kids on the track team for

The Making of "Billie"

a

Decathlete Rafer Johnson coaches Patty Duke in the Billie essentials: running, pole-vaulting and high-jumping. Johnson was the 1960 Olympic gold medalist, after winning a silver in 1956 and a gold in the 1955 Pan American games. He tried his hand in acting, as well, landing small parts in features and television shows.

Patty Duke as "Billie"

HCP051905-5/19/65-HOLLYWOOD: Former world & Olympic decathlon champion Rafer Johnson is over the hurdle with actress Patty Duke right behind him 5/19 as she takes lessons in track & field from the gold medal winner for her upcoming film, "Billie." Miss Duke plays the role of a tomboy teenager who can out-perform any young male athlete on her high school decathlon team. Johnson is the technical advisor for the young Academy Award winner.
UPI TELEPHOTO   hg/cas

about half the roles that paid extras ordinarily would have taken. I suppose it saved the film company some money and made for a lot of happy high school kids... all guys, of course. In that sense, the movie was right on the money. There were no girls on the University High track team. About half the guys on our team were chosen for the film by our coach, Richard Kampmann; I don't know what criteria he used, but he had the undying loyalty of the team. He is now in his eighties and he may today be the coach of the women's track team at Pepperdine University.

"Back then, L.A. schools were not segregated as they are today, with most white kids in private schools and blacks and Latinos and perhaps a majority of Asians in the public schools. My high school, University, served the West L.A. area, and we had the sons of Lloyd Bridges and Burt Lancaster, and at least one daughter of Jeff Chandler on campus. So perhaps it's not so surprising that *Billie* was filmed, in part, at Uni High. I remember, though, how envious other kids on campus were of us.

"I remember marveling over all the uniforms for the two dueling track teams used by us extras. (I'm visible, in my uniform, in one or two scenes, but not recognizable, running over hurdles and milling in the background.) I can remember there were a lot of members of the film crew at Uni High, from cameramen to caterers, the lighting crew, producers, prop and script people, etc. I have a vague memory of delicious lunches on the 'set' and lots of down time between scenes.

"As for the filming itself, I can recall some of it (although now some of the memories are from the point of view portrayed in the film).

"Do you recall Patty zipping around the track after she took the pass? She was belted onto a platform sticking out the back of a pick-up truck, the bed of which was fitted with a moving camera. The truck took a turn around the track with Patty in tow, pumping her arms as if she was running. On the first try, the truck kicked up so much dust that Patty was largely invisible to the camera. It took a while, but I recall a water truck arrived to wet down the track, so neither Patty nor the camera man had to eat dust. In my mind's eye, I can see that truck racing around the track – well, moving slowly around that track – but my main memory comes from the film's point of view, off the back of the truck, looking at Patty/Billie outrunning everyone else on the track, once she got 'The Beat' in her head that gave her the power to perform such amazing feats.

"One of the guys on our track team doubled for Patty in the pole vault. He had to wear a padded bra and a wig and he didn't make any more money than the rest of us, $25 per day. He got a lot of ribbing from the other guys over his willingness for his temporary change of gender.

"The 'regular' double for Patty was indeed an attractive woman, and fairly close to Patty's compact build. I recall little contact with her other than making her (photo) portrait. She was very nice, and I recall she had some difficulty with her accent when she spoke. She really could run the hurdles and, of course, was the real Billie. On the other hand, Patty somehow pulled a muscle just walking around the track, much to the amusement of the guys on our team.

"Patty was cute, lively, and she was friendly. She hung around the set, she ate lunch with the cast and crew, she said hello to the extras, and to me she seemed like a genuinely nice person, which she was and apparently still is. She was not stand-offish, not in the least affected. Living in Southern CA most of my life, I've had a few other brushes with the entertainment business, but none as much fun or as magical as when I was on the set of a real Hollywood movie, with the wonderful Patty Duke."

Billie was completed on time and on budget, as promised by executive producer Lawford. Duke, Weiss and other crew members immediately returned to their regular duties on *The Patty Duke Show*, which was about to enter its third and final season on ABC. Everyone attached to *Billie* was quite proud of what was achieved in a relatively brief period of time, and author Ronald Alexander seemed more than satisfied as the project came to fruition. He watched from the sidelines as his little play blossomed into a pleasing family movie a la Disney, polished up nicely by anamorphic widescreen and three-strip Technicolor photography. "It was harmless, and in those days I did whatever I was told to do," recalls Anna Pearce (PD) today. "I guess the

The Making of "Billie"

Patty Duke's double becomes Billie just long enough to complete the pole-vaulting sequence.

Patty Duke's official, uncredited double, apparently a Swedish athlete, had trouble speaking English. The 'real' Billie, she replaced Duke in all sports-related and dancing sequences for long shots.

original Broadway play was something of a groundbreaker, in that it dealt with women's rights, and this was carried over into the film. For me, it was great just working with some really terrific people."

Patty signs autographs for fans on the set.

The Story

Under Opening Credits

FRESH-FACED CHEERLEADERS SWING INTO ACTION AS A SCHOOLYARD PARADE gains momentum. Carried on the shoulders of high school decathlon runners is a teenage girl wearing an official team tracksuit, weeping what appear to be tears of joy. Who is this celebrated young athlete? The parade's bouncy anthem provides us with a name, and explains how this name defines her:

> *She looks like a Billie should look*
> *Wears her hair like a Billie should wear*
> *She walks like a Billie should*
> *Talks like a Billie should*
> *On her a Billie looks good*
>
> *Her eyes are a Billie-like blue*
> *Her size fits her just like a shoe*

She jumps like a Billie jumps
Runs like a Billie runs
Ain't nothing Billie can't do

She is our teenage queen
Let the others have their king
She makes the world go round
Ain't no one like her around!

She's all that a Billie should be
She just fits her name to a 'T'
Once in a life you find one of a Billie kind
Billie you're the Billie for me!

GG: The self-contained, stylish opening title sequence for *Billie* expresses quite a bit. In an unusual move, this high-energy celebration of our heroine's triumph is a flash-forward to the actual scene, presented in Act Three. That gives the movie an unusual for its time semi-flashback structure, enabling it to start off with an extremely colorful and energetic sequence, while tweaking our interest in general.

We begin with a striking introduction to a boyish-looking pixie of a girl athlete, clearly the day's big winner, being paraded around like a shining trophy. In contrast to the high spirits of the crowd, the young girl weeps. We sense a curious, gentle melancholy that belies the bouncy music.

Reaction shots of all key characters call for extreme mugging to telegraph who is nice and naughty in this family fable (Billy de Wolfe's envious, 'big deal' scowl is most memorable – and it tells us in advance that he's destined to fail). Even Clown the shaggy dog, criticized by some fans for being a four-footed 'laugh track' (his cartoonish reactions replacing canned guffaws, alerting the audience to what's supposedly funny), manages to snag a well-earned, 'single card'-style close-up.

So, in essence, *Billie* sets itself up as an offbeat musical biopic of an imaginary female athlete/local celebrity. We see this teenager in triumph, meet those who were instrumental in her rise and life, and away we go. Perhaps without realizing it, Chrislaw's choice of a title sequence and the subtle flashback structure it initiates unconsciously lend the film a sense of well-mannered importance that, say, Don Weis' next teenage romp, *The Ghost in the Invisible Bikini*, could never hope to achieve. We're not talking *Citizen Kane*, of course. But as many have observed, there is something perversely relevant just below the pop-colored surface of *Billie*, and the movie actually alerts us to this fact from frame one.

CB: Gee, I love movie musicals… especially those great 'coming of age' romantic musical comedies showcasing a feisty girl with plenty of heart, charm and good old-fashioned moxie to spare! Creating the tomboyish title characters in MGM's *Annie Get Your Gun* (1950) and Warner Bros.' *Calamity Jane* (1953), musical comedy superstars Betty Hutton and Doris Day set the bar pretty high for this particular sub-genre.

PATTY DUKE AS "BILLIE"

So how does 1965's *Billie* hold up as a 'coming of age' story? As far as this baby boomer is concerned, right from the opening title sequence it's clear that although the modestly-produced *Billie* may not have been given the lavish Hollywood big budget treatment, this in no way diminishes its charm. That's due in no small measure to the young Academy Award-winner whose talent and 'star quality' shine through from the first frame of film right through to the last. In fact, from the moment we see our heroine bravely fighting back her tears in the midst of a triumphant celebration, Patty Duke as Billie has won our sympathy, even as we assume she's just won some type of sporting competition. (Ironic that the character Billie is being carried on the shoulders of her team, when the success of the movie really rests squarely on the shoulders of its young star!)

On a high school athletic field in Anywhere, USA, we're introduced to the jocks, cheerleaders, and assorted parental units who inhabit Billie's world, in typical musical comedy style. The sound of the marching band and the chorus singing an upbeat anthem to our heroine reminds us of cinematic victory montages past. I'm sure I wasn't the only one reminded of the co-eds and their BMOC partners dancing to the 'Varsity Drag' in the finale of *Good News* (1947) when Peter Lawford's name appeared in the credits (although I may have been the youngest one!).

And one more thing about the credits… the close-up on the actor and then the letters of the name go all psychedelic… groovy, man! I settled back and thought, "This is going to be a fun movie. Gee it would be perfect if only Billie wasn't crying…"

The Story

The Hoyden of Harding High

It's 1965. Welcome to Harding, a small, mostly conservative, all-American suburban community on a blissfully sunny afternoon. Jogging across well-kept grounds and into the Harding High schoolyard is fifteen-and-a-half year old Billie Carol, sheepdog Clown in tow. Energetic Billie enjoys this little warm-up run, and is primed for an afternoon of spirited athletic practice.

Unlike most girls her age, Billie's light blonde hair is cut short and shaped 'page boy' style. She wears a short-sleeved blue valor sweatshirt for casual exercise, matching shorts, and traditional white sneaks.

Usually, the tomboyish youngster wastes little time engaging in workout activities. But today, someone else is busily running and jumping, a boy Billie has never seen before. She patiently watches as this sturdy, determined but sadly unexceptional contender tries some difficult hurdles, only to fall flat on his face. Sympathetic, and looking forward to possibly making a new friend, Billie jogs over.

FIRST IMPRESSIONS OF BILLIE:

GG: Billie presents herself front-and-center, providing a full view of the 1965 model tomboy: the 'bowl cut' hairdo was standard (re: Scout in *To Kill a Mockingbird*), although the form-fitting shorts are a tad sexier than usual. Innocent, bright-eyed, super-energetic, Billie is wholesome Americana personified on the surface, a clean slate...

There are some warning signals for right-of-center thinkers: Both the proto-feminist and gender-bending elements on proud display suggest the beginning of the end of America's patriarchal persona, the start of The Great Unraveling and a supposedly declining U.S. That said, conservatives aren't traditionally anti-tomboy: a feisty and physically strong young woman suggests an equally powerful mother down the line, something heartily welcomed by early settlers anxious to increase the white population.

Patty Duke as "Billie"

The often cute tom is appreciated and accepted, but only if she eventually 'grows out of her awkward phase' and becomes a responsible adult wife and parent. And woe to any misguided female who deviates from this progression.

In any event, Billie is Billie… not some picture perfect Hollywood glamor-puss playing a misfit, but the real deal: a life-loving young woman with glistening eyes and an appealing smile that we take to immediately. Designed to be instantly iconic as a '60s-era tomboy (hairstyle, athletic garb, etc.) and mostly written that way, the character comes to life because of Duke's preternatural empathy. And she hasn't even spoken a word.

By the way, Case… great point about *Good News* and the Peter Lawford connection. Completely forgot about that. *Billie* really did tap into the bouncy style of MGM's culty 1947 school-themed musical. Those *Good News* dancers may not have had The Beat, but they sure had something equally energizing!

When Billie Met Mike

"You new in school?" asks Billie, after introducing herself and a growling Clown to Mike Benson.

"Well my family just moved here last week," he explains.

"Oh. You going out for track?"

"Yeah… Decathlon."

"You'll never make it," Billie tells him frankly, unable to suppress a frown.

Mike's just a little stunned by his new friend's directness. "Well how can you tell?" he asks her.

Billie answers without hesitation. "Your form's all wrong. You get off too slow…"

"Are you the coach?"

"No."

"That's good," observes Mike. He's about to excuse himself from this 'cute' but mildly annoying conversation in order to resume the day's practice.

"No, wait!" Billie interrupts. "You see, the whole secret of speed and elevation is a fast start, drive, kick power… and The Beat."

"The 'Beat'?"

"Uh-huh. You have to *hear* it, up here," the young runner explains, pointing to her forehead, "like this…" Billie snaps her fingers, verbally recreating the sound that accelerates in her head like an engine revving up: "Ba ba ba ba ba ba ba ba ba and *then you go!*"

"Are you sure that's all you hear up there?" asks Mike, bewildered.

"Yeah."

"No strange voices?"

Billie makes a face. "You don't believe me."

"I think you've flipped!"

The teenager ponders this issue of credibility for a moment, then makes a decision. Clearly, a demonstration of the 'Beat' is in order!

The Story

JUST ONE OF THE BOYS, OR IS THERE ROMANCE IN THE AIR?

CB: When it comes to 'boy meets girl' in the movies, you need that 'cute meet' and this is one of the cutest! When Billie meets Mike for the first time, she is still very much an innocent tomboy. She doesn't see him the way other more sophisticated girls her age might: a cute upper-classman, with good looks, a warm, outgoing personality, and the very popular appeal of being 'the new kid in town'. Mike is probably used to shallow females turning on the 'charm' to impress him – but not so with Billie! Meanwhile, she sees Mike as 'one of the boys' and has no problem at all taking him to track school! She has this genuine enthusiasm for sports and wants to help him to run faster and jump higher. Mike is clearly impressed with Billie's quirky ideas – because they work – as evidenced when he stops by her house later that day to ask her to coach him.

This scene shows Billie at her most innocent and child-like. It's important that we see her interacting with Mike in her full-blown 'tomboy' mode because this is the 'before' picture of a girl on the brink of becoming a young woman. We don't doubt for a minute that Mike has had some experience dating girls, but he's never met a girl like her before!

To many of us tween and teen girls, the whole 'Superstar Athlete with The Beat' angle of this movie was just a gimmick – a fun, kinda naughty 'hook' to hang this story on. The real story – the important story – is always… the *love* story.

GG: The introduction of Billie's eventual first boyfriend functions as a slight parody of traditional male-female roles: it's the hunky male athlete who is listening to advice from a teddy bear-like tomboy. Of course Mike thinks Billie has 'flipped', as a) she's just some kid, not the coach, as he rightfully points out, and b) her 'Beat' method sounds eccentric, to say the least. For many leftists, the very presence and early introduction of an attention-splitting romantic interest dilutes what is arguably the most significant aspect of *Billie*, Billie herself. It suggests that chronicling the groundbreaking achievements of a semi-miraculous female athlete wouldn't be 'strong enough' as the subject of a feature film, but putting Billie in the context of a growing-up romance will placate conservative audience members and take the edge off the radical significance of her achievements. Put another way: If she's a tomboy who will eventually be tamed by love and the bliss of traditional wifely behavior, all of Billie's annoying political griping can be forgiven. Amen.

A Woman's Place?

"C'mere," a winsome Billie tells Mike. The two of them, and an equally eager sheepdog, hasten over to the Harding High track for a little high-speed fun. It's the beginning of a much-needed series of field lessons for Mike!

Meanwhile, Mr. Howard P. Carol, Billie's full-of-himself but likeable mayoral-seeking father, is knee deep in a seemingly harmless graduation speech to young high school women.

"…and further, girls of the senior class, the reason that gentility has gone out of our society is, that young ladies are no longer brought up with the grace of my mother, bless her, who brought up my sister, and the way that I'm helping my wife, bring up our two lovely daughters."

Even as he pontificates, one of those lovable daughters is getting ready to run a male opponent into the ground!

The fact that Agnes Carol, also in attendance at the graduation, is wincing at her husband's comments, and half of the listeners are nodding off, seems to completely elude the hale and hearty speaker. Howard blithely delivers what he believes to be a lightweight, non-controversial pep talk supporting young American womanhood, safely reinforcing traditional family values.

"…and it is a sad comment that women have come from parasols in the garden, to bikinis on the beach…"

Wearing shorts that are almost as revealing as a bikini, and sneakers instead of designated track shoes, Billie positions herself at the runners' starting line. Mike Benson's on the outside, Clown's right beside her. And as she conjures the super-energizing Beat in her head, it fills the girl's body and soul with a confidence so intense, so supremely satisfying that soon she's beaming from ear-to-ear!

"...and what is even worse, women have been forced to compete with men, and may I say they are not happy being placed in that position."

A second later Billie's off like a rocket. Trying to keep up, Mike watches in awe as this young female aces him on the hurdles, lightning-fast legs running, leaping, then running again, and leaping again. Billie follows this dazzling display with some spectacular high jumps over a raised bar. In a word, WOW!

"...and so, in closing, this competition between boys and girls has warped the position of young ladies in society. The fault is not with you, it is with our generation."

AN EARLY '50s SOCIAL MINDSET IN THE MID-'60s:

GG: Howard's social views about women and the family were deliberately stale and ridiculous even in the '50s, when Ronald Alexander first penned them; in the '60s, they are high camp, and the movie fully knows it (bored and eye-rolling reactions, cross-cutting to his own daughter making mincemeat of these quaint views). One suspects even Howard is aware of this, and was simply coasting on a fluffy bit of sexist nostalgia without considering the consequences.

CB: Don't be fooled by the attempts to cast aspersions on Billie's father Howard! He is a complex, intelligent, competent role model who more than deserves his place of honor as graduation speaker. Less sophisticated viewers might not see beyond the obvious comic elements of cutting back and forth from his thoughtful speech and the antics of his tomboy daughter. Those viewers have missed the point completely! Billie, racing for her new 'buddy' at the track, is acting in an age-appropriate manner for a fifteen-year-old high school sophomore. Howard P. Carol's speech extolling the virtues of gentility,

Patty Duke as "Billie"

cooperation and shared responsibility between husbands and wives is being given to graduating seniors – young women who have surely outgrown their 'tomboy' ways!

Statistically speaking, many of these seniors have already been 'pinned' and are going steady with the young men that they will soon marry. For goodness sake, some are already engaged! Rather than talking down to them, Mr. Carol addresses them as they are: responsible young women on the brink of marriage and motherhood (Bravo, and pass me one of those ubiquitous campaign buttons, Mr. C.!).

On a side note, I thoroughly and completely believe that one of the greatest directors of all time shared my esteem for the character of Howard P. Carol! Consider the possibility that our cinematic introduction to Howard was the visual template that Francis Ford Coppola unconsciously channeled when filming his introduction of Michael Corleone in the iconic 'baptism/execution' scene in *The Godfather* (1972). Note how Coppola mirrors the juxtaposition of text and images in his homage to Don Weis' original 'graduation/track race' montage.

GG: Howard's 'thoughtful' speech? The one about women and parasols? Is that why his wife Agnes, soon to be established as the movie's voice of reason, looks like she's going to throw up as he's delivering it?

CB: She simply looks embarrassed.

GG: Also, with all due respect, Francis Ford Coppola's 'homage' to Don Weis is a tad hard to accept. Ironic cross-cutting has been around since the silent era.

CB: I was joking.

GG: I knew that.

MIKE BENSON'S REACTION TO BILLIE:

GG: His ego intact after being outclassed, the male hero seems amazed and delighted to have such a skillful new athletic companion. At this stage of their relationship, Billie could have just as easily been Billy, a young boy that affable Mike Benson befriends, races with and learns from. She is boyish-looking enough that he may have actually mistaken her for one at first (dialogue is not gender-specific during this initial encounter).

Nice Guys and a Jerky Jock

Billie and Mike finish their last lap just as the Harding High running team races by. "Hi, Ted!" shouts a cheerful Billie, clearly fond of these local boys who share her sporty interests.

All but one, that is… the team's Captain, a muscular, good-looking but somewhat immature jock named Eddie Davis. He's the son of Mayor Davis, currently running for re-election against challenger Howard Carol. Billie makes the intros, and Davis seems amused by Mike Benson's goal of decathlon victory. And just why is that?

"I saw you working out with Billie here, and I kinda had you figured for varsity hop scotch," he says snidely.

"Oh you better watch out for him, Mike," Billie chimes in. "He's a big four letter man: B-O-R-E."

A laughing Mike certainly appreciates the humor in this. Even the other runners can't help grinning at their little gal pal's moxie.

But Eddie isn't smiling. "Oh, why don't you beat it, kid," he snorts.

"Make me!"

With that, Billie takes off down the track, Clown maintaining her pace. And giving all he's got in a chase he never should have taken the bait for, Eddie Davis, Captain of the celebrated Harding High track team, trails far, far behind Billie Carol.

Then, even *farther* behind.

Until he's so far in the distance the joke's totally on him. At one point, a pleased-as-punch Billie actually stops, turns, places her hands on her hips and practically taps her foot impatiently as she gives hapless Eddie extra time to catch up. Then she's off again, widening the distance between them even more.

At that very moment Coach Jones and some of the other team members happen to be entering the field. Though this chase between Davis and his blonde quarry is a far distance off, Billie's amazing running prowess catches the coach's eye.

"Who's that boy?" he asks the others.

"That's no boy, coach... that's a girl!"

A few seconds later this girl zooms past them at what can only be described as hyper-reality speed. All heads turn instantly from left to right as she streaks by.

"I don't believe it," Coach Jones admits aloud, eyes still trained on a now-vanishing Billie. Then he motions to the stunned students he's with. "Get her and bring her back," he orders them. "I don't care if you have to do it in relays!"

The guys take off after Billie. And the Beat Girl's arrogant antagonist/pursuer, winded and finally in the vicinity, is called over by Coach Jones.

"Who was that rocket you were following?" Jones asks 'Captain' Davis.

"Ah, some kid."

"Either you're in terrible condition, or she should be running at Churchill Downs."

"I could've caught her any time I wanted to," whines Eddie.

"So why didn't you?" is the logical next question.

"Oh, uh… her dog kept getting in the way!"

This feeble excuse doesn't fly. Recognizing a genuine phenom when he sees one, Coach Davis starts making plans for an unlikely new running champion…

BILLIE'S RELATIONSHIP WITH FELLOW HARDING ATHLETES:

CB: These noble young scholar-athletes (so often denounced as 'mindless jocks') had signed up for an all-male team in good faith, but soon proved they would put personal feelings of impropriety aside for the good of the team. The boys show that Harding school spirit and will soon get behind adding Billie to the team roster because she will help lead their school to victory!

GG: Billie seems to have a happy, non-threatening friendship with most of the macho guys who race at Harding. This is mainly because she's a likeable lass who shares their interests, but also because they simply don't take her seriously as a competitor. These decent-enough jocks really aren't to blame: they've never seen a girl compete with a guy athletically, let alone best him decisively. They've been conditioned to think of all women as demure, delicate creatures. Being alpha male athletes, they are simply doing what comes naturally in a comfortably sexist 1965 America that legally and psychologically discourages females from reaching their full potential. To their credit as athletes, these guys recognize and respect athletic prowess in a woman when it's finally demonstrated to them. Why they hadn't noticed field regular Billie's extraordinary gifts before is anyone's guess.

CB: They know what Billie knows – that elite athletes compete first and foremost against their own best teams, and then against opposing teams – not against each other!

TELLING OFF A BULLY:

CB: Interestingly enough, in the movies where the tomboyish heroine is older than Billie, she will usually engage in banter with her leading man as a 'battle of the sexes' begins. In the world of musical comedy this gave us memorable duets such as "Anything You Can Do (I Can Do Better)" by Annie Oakley and Frank Butler and "I Can Do Without You" by Calamity Jane and Bill Hickok. The sexual tension is palpable between these soon-to-be lovers as they engage in their energetic game of one-upmanship! The audience knows that all passionate rivalry will eventually morph into passion of a romantic nature, even if the rivals aren't aware of it yet. There is no similar interplay between Billie and her rival, Eddie Davis, because she has yet to feel the stirrings of those 'funny little butterflies' in her tummy. That will come later, and with Billie's real leading man, Mike.

GG: Representing the challenged alpha male, Eddie Davis is *Billie*'s second villain (his slimy dad, the Mayor, is the first). Although Eddie's intolerance of Billie's very existence seems a little on the nose, it's an accurate reflection of the mean-spirited resentment many small-minded jocks felt toward the emerging female athlete back in the 60s and 70s. When Eddie calls Billie a 'kid', which is objectively a reasonable way to categorize someone of her age and appearance, it nevertheless puts the young woman down as someone not worth taking seriously. She's simply a silly tomboy having problems growing up, a mild irritant to genuine, male athletes like himself. In real life, most likely, Billie would have outperformed Eddie several times already, making his overly-confident tomboy chase a little implausible... but in movie reality, the 'surprise' of this young girl's astonishing skill needed to be dramatized, just as it was demonstrated for newcomer/audience representative Mike Benson. On the intellectual front, Billie is clearly Davis' superior, responding to his uninspired insults with clever, well-delivered retorts. And when she tricks Eddie into chasing her and winds up making a fool of him (in front of the coach, no less), it's obvious she's ahead of this game in just about every way possible.

CB: Absolutely. Billie doesn't know it yet, but in Mike Benson she's just met her own future alpha male. The fact that the sparks don't fly immediately between them is a radical departure from the usual *Taming of the Shrew* formula, but makes perfect sense in the context of a coming-of-age romance. It will take a far better man than obnoxious Eddie to awaken the woman in Billie and turn her from tomboy to teenager in love!

GG: Throwing us a curve as always, author Ronald Alexander has Billie/Ginger actually marrying Eddie Davis in his sequel to *Time Out for Ginger*, *Time and Ginger* (1980). So he actually followed through with the 'battle of the sexes' scenario set up between Billie and Eddie, neatly transferring this fight to Billie and frustrated Mike Benson (who soon wants Billie off the track, just like jealous Eddie does) for the 1965 movie.

CB: Wow. Eddie and Billie wind up together?

GG: He's on the receiving end of her scathing wit every step of the way, just like when they were kids. But the romantic comedy circle is complete.

FANTASY SPEED... ENDEARING OR PATRONIZING?

GG: The Beat amounts to a cute but cartoonish and ultimately condescending method of showing how an athlete revs up for maximum performance. No one's denying the importance of mental preparation, and the driving beat of rock and roll music is not a bad way to convey Billie's process of summoning energy. But the regrettable truth is, Alexander and company decided that a female athlete must have what plays as a fanciful super-power in order to justify beating boy runners, even if that power is actually nothing more than a personal way of marshaling inner confidence. It's just far easier for traditionalists to accept female physical prowess if these skills are presented as some kind of pseudo-fantasy asset. Ridiculously enough, girls defeating boys through sheer athletic superiority needed tempering for the sake of 'credibility' in these socially primitive, pre-Billie Jean King days.

CB: "Billie's Got The Beat!" as the movie trailer proclaimed, and what a beat it is! In the hands of a lesser actress, this crucial plot element might have devolved into a gimmick, but Patty Duke has the skill to convince us that she's 'hearing' what the audience is literally hearing: the driving percussion in 4/4 that fuels her character's quest for speed.

Sure, we hear the soundtrack, and it's a cool, catchy 'four on the floor' rock & roll drum riff! But that isn't enough. It's the way that we're shown how Billie 'hears' and then 'feels' The Beat that is so much fun for the audience! Maybe it was more visceral for a girl like me who would later become a drummer and percussion teacher, but it felt like every girl who was watching Billie psyche herself up to The Beat was energized right along with her!

Now there will be some misguided (probably non-athletic) types who will dismiss The Beat as a way of diminishing Billie's athletic prowess. Predictably, they overstate the obvious physicality of athletics while underestimating the importance of the mental preparation – especially for the athlete who must overcome a less-than-optimal body type for a chosen sport. Let's get real! Our heroine does not have the ideal body type to compete in track and field events. Does this mean she should give up? Hell, no! It just means that she needs to optimize all of her assets – physical and mental – and find a way to create a winning strategy.

That strategy is The Beat – her innovative, way ahead-of-its-time precursor to many currently well-respected sports performance optimization techniques that often include an element of rhythm. Collectively, these mental preparation activities like visualization, chanting, meditation and biofeedback are used as aids to bring athletes into 'The Zone'. Today's elite professional athletes often resemble Billie listening to The Beat as they enter 'The Zone' – a real life, empirically proven mind/body connection that turns 'performance' to 'super performance'.

GG: Why am I not surprised that you're groovin' to The Beat? You're a professional musician and music teacher who sure as hell knows her stuff! Love those parallels to real-world studies of athletes using rhythm training to enter 'The Zone' and improve their performance, and the delicate way you mentioned how a girl of Billie's un-trim body type would require extra mental/discipline training to compensate. My big Beat problem is overly fanciful presentation, and the unfortunate social message this conveys, which, IMO, outweighs any sports preparation-related benefits. It's offered up as something inexplicable and almost mystical, like a power Billie might have received from a fairy godmother. Normal confidence-building psychological prepping would NEVER be enough to enable a female athlete to triumph over a male, this '65 movie seems to be saying. So instead of presenting Billie's unique process of mental discipline in realistic terms, putting her on equal footing with more heavy-duty male competitors, she seems blessed with The Beat the way a Jedi Knight is strong with the Force.

Oh, and by the way, I shoot a pretty mean game of pool.

CB: So do I.

GG: Check.

CB: And I happen to think the glass is half-full here. The Beat is an intriguing, innovative way to show how mental preparation works, and how it can make a difference. It's one of the most distinctive things about *Billie*.

GG: You realize that only Alexander's Billie has 'The Beat'. All of his

Gingers were Beatless, and, in terms of credibility, probably better for it. But Duke is such a terrific actress she sells this far-fetched mental discipline, you're absolutely right about that. In another era, she'd be playing an X-Men mutant, in angst over a unique power that seems to piss off and intimidate the traditionalists around her.

By the way, the Beat theme (and the entire *Billie* score, for that matter) was provided by Dominic Frontiere, perhaps best known to film/TV music buffs as the composer of *The Outer Limits*.

CB: No shit. It sounds altogether different. But that's as it should be, given the subject matter.

GG: And *The Patty Duke Show* was running on ABC at the same time as *Limits*; both were UA-TV series. Would've made for a funny crossover if *TPDS* did an Orson Welles "War of The Worlds" episode, with Patty and even initially-skeptical Cathy Lane trying to convince their newspaper editor dad that Martians have landed (cue one of *OL*'s resident bogeys making a guest appearance).

CB: Those alien monsters wouldn't stand a chance against the Lane cousins!

GG. Frontiere's *Billie* score came out on CD a year or so ago. It offers the same musical cues that were on the original 1965 vinyl LP, which is still available on eBay.

Growing Pains

The comfortable, suburban home of the Carols is aglow with joy as daughter Jeannie arrives unexpectedly. Twenty years old and ultra-feminine, she's very much the antithesis of her boyish sister Billie. It appears Jeannie's quitting college and returning home for good, a decision her delighted father, the self-proclaimed next mayor of Harding, heartily endorses. On the other hand, Agnes isn't so sure this is for the best. "I think it's something we should discuss," she tells Jeannie with some concern. And then there's Bob Matthews, Jeannie's old beau and perennial fiancé, finishing up his final year at Harvard. How does he fit into her sudden change of plan?

Howard laughs, casually admits to being an "old fashioned, possessive father" when it comes to his daughter's social life. He worries about Jeannie's future romantic entanglements... but not Billie's, he explains to Agnes with a chuckle. "At the rate she's going no young man will be able to catch her, and even if he could he wouldn't be able to hold her unless he's a professional wrestler!"

Ding-dong.

Enter a post-workout Mike Benson, who shows up at the front door asking to see Billie. Young Benson appears to be a nice enough, well-mannered fellow, but dating a fifteen-year-old tomboy like Billie? "I don't want to date her, I want her as a teacher," Mike explains to a befuddled Howard. He further explains that he was equally hard to convince, at first...

"...until she beat me at the 100-yard dash, the high jump, the long jump, the 220, the 440..."

"How'd you make out in the shot put?"

"I was afraid to try, sir."

Right. Just then Billie romps into the house, and she's delighted to see that her new friend Mike has stopped over. He chuckles admiringly at her remarkable athletic skill, but Howard's hardly amused. "It's bad enough that we're ruled from cradle to grave by women..." Howard shouts to two very quiet and respectful listeners. "But if they're going to start becoming sports managers and coaches for men, well, that is the last straw!" he bellows.

"One mustn't stand in the way of progress, sir... no matter what form it takes," protests Mike with gumption. Billie looks at her new pal and beams, impressed that he's turning out to be a kindred spirit in a number of ways. But after she agrees to coach Mike and the young man finally says his goodbyes, Howard does his best to 'set his daughter straight' with a minimum of melodrama.

"From now on, try to remember that you're a girl," he says more pragmatically than forcefully.

Billie shakes her head, knowing they're on the same inner wavelength. "I wish I was a boy."

"Well so do I, but you're not!"

Wham. The fifteen-year-old takes this last statement hard. And Howard's follow-up suggestion that Billie emulate her older sister's ladylike demeanor is met with the usual reluctant nod of daughterly assurance. Or resignation.

"Daddy? Do you love me?" Billie finally asks, her eyes needful and moist.

"Of course I love you," is Howard's earnest, somewhat pained response.

"I'm glad. Because you're really going to have to."

Howard isn't quite sure what that statement means. And maybe Billie isn't, either.

Alone in her room, away from an outwardly sunny world that doesn't understand square pegs, a crestfallen Billie looks at childhood playthings. And feels just about as removed from reality as they are…

I feel just like a toy, my head is in a whirl.
I should have been a boy but here I am a girl.
What good is growing up when this is all it means?
I'm an in-between, a lonely little in-between.

I don't have fun on dates, I feel so out of place.
The boys don't act the same as when we're in a race.
I just can't be myself, at least that's how it seems.
I'm an in-between, a lonely little in-between.

My father loves me so and I adore him, too.
Why can't he understand the heartaches I am going through?

The Story

I don't know who to please, why can't I just be me?
I'm sitting on a fence, confused as I can be.
Sometimes it really hurts just to be fifteen,
And an in-between, a lonely little in-between,
That's me.

Unable to change her situation, at least at the moment, Billie sighs. She's torn between sneakers and that bottle of perfume… a tomboy at the crossroads.

JEANNIE AS THE IDEAL '60s ROLE MODEL:

GG: The character of Jeannie exists to show us what a 'normal' 1965 American girl is all about, in contrast to the plush-toy unreality of her living tomboy cartoon character sister. Smart enough for college, Jeannie's more than happy to chuck higher learning and a future of individual accomplishment for the bliss of serving future husband Don Hollinger. A comfortable future with a decent enough slice of white bread represented the American female dream during this period, with Jeannie providing the recommended blend of pertness, femininity, resourcefulness (she's a master architect of crazy fibbing), and logical 'sense of proper place'… in the shadow of her husband, of course.

Patty Duke as "Billie"

The Carol sisters, Jeannie and Billie.

CB: The character of Jeannie exists to show us yet another facet of Billie's personality: her love of family! These are sisters who clearly love and respect each other, and more – they *like* each other. (Of course the mutual admiration society scales may tip a bit more in the direction of kid sister adoration of big sister – but speaking from experience I can categorically assert there's no person on planet Earth cooler to a fifteen-year-old than her amazing college-age sister!)

But hey – let's acknowledge that Jeannie is cool in her own right! Let's not forget that, in the big picture, Billie ran around a track a few times as her big 'rebellion'. Jeannie, on the other hand, managed to stay in college until her secret elopement and subsequent pregnancy made it impractical. She had the gumption to know what and who she wanted – she is the original 'follow your bliss' girl!

Will she succeed as wife and mother? No way to tell for sure – but at least the decision to try was hers and hers alone. Will there be so-called feminists who will try to belittle their choices? Certainly! But the *true* feminist viewpoint should be 'Free to choose your own life' not 'Free to finish college and get a job outside the home'.

(Oh, please let me add an update on that amazing sister that I referenced earlier. Like Jeannie, she married her college sweetheart (45th wedding anniversary coming up), was a stay-at-home mom who nurtured four great kids and returned to college for a Master's Degree and a mid-life career as a beloved special ed. teacher after her youngest child was in school full time. Yup, she is *still* the coolest person on planet Earth!)

GG: And just as addicted to dancing as you are… talk about The Beat!

You're right on target about Billie and her sister Jeannie; more about their happy relationship in an upcoming scene. As for Jeannie's freedom of choice, let's just say that everything's relative, and that her life choices are made through the prism of what's considered socially acceptable for women in 1965 America. That's why it's so easy for her to abandon the benefits of higher learning and hitch herself to a well-to-do husband, something enthusiastically encouraged by her father… and rightfully questioned by a concerned Agnes Carol, certainly the most mature and progressive member of this family.

"Bark! Bark!!" Sorry, Clown, but you *were* included in that evaluation.

HOWARD'S CHRONIC CHAUVINISM/MIKE'S INHERENT LIBERALISM:

CB: Mike is appropriately deferential to adults, as befits a well-mannered teenager in a small town in the mid 1960s. But, like Billie, he has the courage of his convictions and is certainly not shy about expressing himself. This scene has little to do with Howard Carol's opinions – but is crucial in establishing Mike as a worthy object of our young heroine's very first crush.

GG: More an easy 'old vs. new' comedy device than a political comment, fuddy duddy Howard is flustered by social progress, while modern-thinking Mike happily embraces it. To a point. He hasn't fallen in love with Billie yet. She's just a genderless buddy and teacher, although one suspects those always-on-display gams are beginning to have an effect. At the moment, as a progressive 'anti-father', Mike appears to be ten feet tall in Billie's eyes, which shine in approval.

BILLIE AND HOWARD'S BOY WISH/WHAT'S BEHIND "YOU'RE GONNA HAVE TO":

GG: The most memorable exchange in this movie has Billie deeply regretting the fact that she wasn't born a boy (echoes of Jo from *Little Women*), her father harshly agreeing and showing frustration at an unkind fate, and the girl's justifiable "Do you love me?" follow-up question. The inevitable "Of course I do" is answered by the line that many in the gay community feel foreshadows the trials ahead once Billie officially outs herself: "I'm glad… because you're really going to have to." However you read this, it's a sad, desperate warning that every belief her father considers rock-solid is about to be questioned/possibly shattered, and that Howard's true feelings for his daughter will indeed be tested even as his pride takes an unavoidable beating.

CB: Pshaw! Speaking as the person who actually *was* a little girl, I can tell you that Billie didn't mean it when she said she wanted to *be* a boy. What she actually meant was she wanted to be able to *act* like a boy. Only a man would blow her comment, and her father's, so out of proportion. Back in the childhood days of this era, 'boys" games were far more exciting and physically challenging than 'girls" games. Billie's father understands why she'd prefer these endeavors, but he realizes that soon she'll be growing up and leaving her innocent years behind. His only fault is that he encouraged her to remain a tomboy for a bit longer than usual. Now even he can see that Billie has stayed too long at the 'boy world' fair, which is why he's encouraging her to move forward to the next developmental step.

GG: But why can't the next developmental step be a record-shattering career in the Olympics, along with managing a happy social life that doesn't necessarily involve a marriage, or even a steady male-female relationship? And what if Billie actually *is* gay? Should the father of another Billie (Jean King) have encouraged his daughter to 'grow out' of her 'tomboy obsessions' and mature into a traditional, man-serving housewife? Not that there's anything wrong with that, as Mr. Seinfeld might say… but other options exist, and many believe it's a sin to waste such exceptional talent.

Rebel with a Cause

It's been quite a day for visitors at the Carol residence. Now, Arnold Wilson shows up… and he's in a huff.

"Howard, I've been principal at Harding High for 23 years," he explains dutifully, before dropping a bombshell. "This afternoon Billie went out for the track team!"

"The boy's track team?"

"That's the only kind we have. The coach says she runs like a gazelle and jumps like a kangaroo. He was going to use her to shame the boys into trying harder."

Caught by surprise, Howard's at a loss. "Can't you declare the girls ineligible?"

"On what grounds?" Agnes chimes in, silent up to now but certainly interested in where this conversation is going. "I'm not defending her, I'm just asking."

After cautioning his wife about "talking that way in front of her," Howard finally calls his daughter downstairs.

"Now what is this foolishness about you trying out for the boys' track team?" he demands to know.

"Well the coach asked me to."

"Well you're not going to do it!" Howard proclaims steadfastly.

Billie seems a little thrown by this no-room-for-discussion order. "I'm not?"

"Darling, it is a strenuous sport for a girl," sympathetic but concerned Agnes interjects.

"Not for me, Mom! I've got The Beat!" Bright-eyed Billie retorts, blissfully snapping her fingers and boppin' to that special inner rhythm.

"Young lady, you're going to force me to pass a regulation prohibiting girls from partaking in *any* sport," threatens the perturbed school principal.

And that crosses the line, as far as Billie is concerned.

"Mr. Wilson, if I'm denied my athletic rights I'll refuse to attend classes," she tells him, straight-faced.

Wilson is more than a little flustered. "I'll have you expelled!" he snarls.

"But sir," well-mannered Billie explains, her strident tone relenting a tad.

"The Constitution and the Bill of Rights guarantee every American citizen life, liberty and the pursuit of happiness…"

In spite of everything, Howard beams with pride, although Billie doesn't notice this reaction. "Some of her arguments make a good deal of sense," he later tells Wilson. "What does the coach think?"

"We don't pay the coach to think. We pay the coach to teach English."

All too true. Mind made up, a defiant Howard states that "if Billie thinks she can make that boys' team, then she should be allowed to try it." He's actually quite delighted with the way his daughter stood up to stuffy Principal Wilson, defending personal rights and social justice like a pint-sized Clarence Darrow. Unfortunately, while happily pondering Billie's athletic possibilities ("I wonder if she is part gazelle…"), he is reminded by Agnes about a certain little speech he recently gave about a woman's place in society.

Looks like it's going to be a long election!

CASUAL DISREGARD FOR FEMALE ATHLETICS:

CB: In this scene, Principal Wilson functions as 'The Man We Love to Hate'. Written in broad strokes, we know that his character is just a foil. As principal he can, if you'll pardon the expression, stop Billie in her tracks. That alone would be more than enough to qualify him for villain status.

GG: As *Billie* is essentially a big screen sitcom, characters are exaggerated and stereotypical (crusty old coach, befuddled principal… Billie herself), and one accepts this stylization or doesn't bother to watch. That said, hearing a High School principal threatening to abolish female athletics is nothing less than grotesque to modern viewers, something akin to Nazi doctrine or Old South slavery. Granted, the upset character is clearly over-reacting, or possibly using fear tactics on Billie by threatening a ban he would never seriously consider implementing.

Patty Duke as "Billie"

RATIONAL AND RESPECTFUL TONE OF BILLIE'S DEFIANCE:

GG: Without missing a beat, if you'll pardon the expression, the movie has Billie respond to the principal's freedom-crushing threat with commendable edge for 1965, smartly slipping back into super-respectful 'But, sir' mode after the intelligence of her argument has won the debate. Billie's future as a great leader in the liberal-progressive wing of the Democratic Party seems all but assured.

CB: Billie's respectful tone can be traced back to the way she was raised by her loving parents, Agnes and Howard. They have raised both Jeannie and Billie to think for themselves and express their opinions with courtesy and civility.

It may be true that father rather than mother might have been more influential in molding their feisty, can-do attitudes. However, it's clear that both young women have been taught good manners and have had an exquisite role model for sure in the person of Agnes Carol. Close scrutiny of this scene reveals that Billie, like her mother, has a sharp mind but a kind tongue.

Oh yes, there's one other thing that we need to remember about Billie as the 'good girl'. She may be fifteen years old chronologically, but she has yet to enter the rebellious teenage years, personality-wise. When she does… watch out!

GG: Exactly. No doubt in my mind that Billie Carol becomes a sitar-playing, fully-committed student protester a few years after the events of this film.

HOWARD'S BUDDING ENLIGHTENMENT:

CB: My 8th grade glass proverb was: "Show me your companions and I'll tell you who you are."
Howard Carol is surrounded by smart, sassy women who absolutely adore him! Is his warm heart somewhat camouflaged by a curmudgeonly exterior? Why, yes it is. But when it matters, he can be counted on to do the right thing. He is, in a word, a mensch. If he wasn't, how could he hope to keep the affection of his terrific wife Agnes and respect of his amazing daughters?

GG: After setting up Howard Carol as a lovable but backward-thinking ass, it's important for *Billie* to show this character's relative maturity once things start getting serious. After all, why should we care for/respect Billie if her heartfelt quest is to win the approval of a father not worthy of her?
The product of a complacent, unconsciously sexist society, Howard Carol is as guilty as any apathetic white male who allowed unfair practices to thrive during his watch. Perhaps he will make use of his burgeoning enlightenment and fight for positive change, if he wins the election. We're pleased to see signs here that the old-fashioned political blowhard is sane enough to recognize right from wrong, and extreme right from reasonable left, when it truly counts.

CB: Mr. Magoo Goes to Washington!

GG: ...and the women in his life will keep him honest! Here's to First Lady Agnes.

CB: Let's elect her President instead! I've got the perfect campaign slogan: May The Beat Be with You!

The Progressive Parent

The Carols, along with Howard's mayoral campaign manager Matt Bullitt, cheer Billie on as she competes against heavy-duty male opponents in the track team try-outs. Strenuous athletic challenges of the day include pole-vaulting and shot-putting, along with high-speed running.

Scheming Mayor Davis saunters over to Howard's family, flashing his best snake charmer smile. Davis casually suggests that he and Howard engage in a series of public debates ("Everybody does it"), clearly hoping to embarrass his opponent with Billie's gender-bending endeavors on the sports field. Howard accepts, his manager realizing full well what Harding's shifty major is up to.

Meanwhile, Billie uses her inner Beat to race far ahead of all the boys. They pump and piston mightily but simply can't match this teen girl's lightning speed. And Howard Carol couldn't be more delighted. He may have wanted a boy, but what he got instead is certainly filling him with a father's pride.

Coming in second, and with a lot of coaching from his femme trainer, Mike Benson starts shaping up as a decent athlete himself. But it's Billie's show all the way... and the local crowd goes wild!

Dazzled by her spectacular athletic performance, Billie's family visits the Harding High locker room to congratulate her for making the team. Coach Davis promptly directs the Carols to her impromptu dressing room, a sports equipment storage facility fixed up rather sweetly by the boys.

But despite her significant victory, Billie is anything but pleased. As a matter of fact, "I'm boiling, just boiling!" she tells her surprised parents. "Mom, they're making fun of me."

"How do you know that?" Howard asks.

"They treat me like a girl, and not an equal!"

"But darling, you are a girl…" Agnes reminds her.

"I don't care. I want to be an equal first!" Billie insists, frustrated by the apparently unintentional condescension of the males in her midst.

Howard shrugs, trying to put the best face on his daughter's dissatisfaction. "She's discovered a whole new sex," he says philosophically. "Boys, girls, and equals!"

Early that evening, Mike stops over for his usual Beat lesson. As rock and roll music scores her actions, blissful Billie demonstrates some fluid moves by dancing around and about the seated teenage boy. Benson is way quieter than usual, and certainly quieter than family dog Clown, who growls knowingly at his lame attempt at a friendly smile.

Suddenly and unexpectedly, Billie has become more than merely a tomboyish youngster who can outrun and outplay him, Mike realizes. She's a girl and she's cute and she knows how to work her Beat-enlivened teenage body. Billie, on the other hand, seems completely oblivious to her friend's personal dilemma. Left open-mouthed after he takes off for a figurative cold shower, she continues her musically-driven exercises… this time with Clown for a dancing partner!

A short while later, Jeannie and Billie are waiting for Mike to pick them up for tonight's town hall debate. The twenty-year-old, elusive about where things stand with longtime beau Bob Matthews, finally fesses all to little sis: they were married seven months ago! Jeannie's just been waiting for a less frenetic time to tell her loving parents. Wilder still, she came back home because she thinks she's having a baby. "Ho, ho, ho, and a half," is all a stunned Billie can say in response to that little bombshell.

"So you see, it's a good thing you're not more like me," Jeannie grins with good-natured resignation.

"Yeah," laughs Billie. "If I was, sister dear, Daddy'd kill both of us!"

Whoops... The siblings look at each other for a held moment, their happy smiles gradually fading.

Less than an hour later, the Carol-Davis town hall debate is in full swing. As expected, Billie's unconventional track pursuits are grist for the local political mill, especially given Howard's recent views on the subject of male and female roles in society.

"Do you approve of your daughter being on the boys' track team?" a bemused audience member asks him.

"No, not particularly."

"Then why don't you get her off?"

"Well, as a good progressive parent, I don't think I should stand in her way."

That's all the opening Mayor Davis requires. "If you carry your so-called 'progressive' ideas into politics, our entire social structure could become a bedlam, in no time at all!" he proclaims, to surprisingly loud applause.

For the first time, Howard seems to be at a loss for words. And Billie, watching with sympathetic eyes, begins to understand what the noble cause of fighting for Equal Rights may cost her father.

SUPERSTAR ATHLETE OR FREAK ATTRACTION/"EQUAL FIRST":

GG: While it's understandable that speed demon Billie would be perceived as a novelty, the girl's frustration is palpable and fully justified: an 'Equal First, Girl Second' theme is introduced here, soon to become Billie's mantra and passionate battle cry. There's little question this smart young lady understands on a gut level what the score is; at least initially, she's chosen the progressive intellectual route, rightfully demanding full rights as a human being before being classified as a slightly sub-human species by the socially unenlightened society she happens to be a part of.

CB: The controversy arises not because Billie is a phenom, but because

she will be competing against boys. If there was a girls' team, she would be the superstar of that team and on her way to a full college scholarship.

Billie, help is on the way; if not for you, then surely for your daughters. It's called 'Title IX'.

SISTERS: DIFFERENT AS NIGHT AND DAY:

CB: Much of these superficial differences are due to the fact that Jeannie is a grown woman while Billie is essentially still a child. But in one way they are alike: in their love for each other and their family.

GG: Obviously important for the 'correct' and 'incorrect' female symbols they represent. But as the plot doesn't require pitting one sister against another, opposites Jeannie and Billie enjoy and seem to have always enjoyed a charmingly caring, totally honest and nonjudgmental relationship with each other.

IS BILLIE COMPLETELY INNOCENT AND OBLIVIOUS AS SHE 'TEASES' MIKE:

CB: Yes.

GG: On the surface, Patty Duke plays the moment with total innocence. Still... are natural feelings of arousal dovetailing with Beat energy as she slinks about to spirited rock music, hapless Mike clearly under her spell? Is our gosh-honest teddy bear tomboy destined to become just another conniving (like her sister), predatory, man-manipulating female? Are sly-as-the-devil feminine wiles an uncontested reality, even in the most chaste and tomboyish female youngster?

Not from where this popcorn-chomping viewer is sitting, nope. Although the idea of inherently honest Billie discovering, much to her bemusement, the practical benefits of romantic manipulation, and eventually making use of seductive wiles for constructive purposes, does indeed boggle the mind.

She'd probably go easy on nice guy Mike. But future hubby Eddie Davis, her erstwhile sexist adversary during childhood, is going to have quite a marathon ahead of him...

WHAT'S UP WITH THE DOG DANCE?

GG: Patty Duke needed a stunt double for her little dance with Clown. It was never considered to be anything other than a sweet moment, but the decision to shoot it in semi-dark long shot (partially to hide the fact that a stand-in's being used) lends it creepy overtones to some people who seem anxious to link Billie's radically 'boyish' behavior with sexual deviancy. "First tomboys, then lesbians, finally sex with animals... it's Ancient Rome falling all over again," the right-wingers warn us, ignoring an avalanche of inconvenient truths that blow apart this bizarre analogy.

CB: This gentle moment foreshadows the end of Billie's childhood, and the bittersweet beginnings of first love. In the prior scene, those close-ups of Billie's pert derriere are the camera's way of showing us where Mike is looking. It's reminiscent of the moment when Gaston asks himself the musical question: "When did your sparkle turn to fire?" as he realizes Gigi has grown from a gamin into a lovely young woman, so Mike realizes that he no longer views Billie as just a friend. He does the gentlemanly thing and leaves childlike Billie to her 'playground', then heads off to figure out how he's going to proceed. A little confused by this abrupt departure, Billie turns to her dog for an impromptu dance, something she's probably done a thousand times before.

Clown is very special – he's always there for Billie as running partner, shoulder to cry on and all-around best friend. But Clown also serves as a symbol of Ms. Carol's childhood. This is her last dance in the land of make-believe, where little girls and their dogs are dancing partners. Sigh…

GG: Years later, Peter Jackson would tap into the same theme for his Ann Darrow-King Kong relationship… innocence is indeed 'beautiful' as Ann and Kong watch sunsets together, but sooner or later this woman must accept adult life's risks and take a chance with a real companion. Ann/Billie begins to realize that she must put childhood pets and pleasures aside for something even greater, but without ever forgetting how important they were to her emotional stability. Sigh…

CB: YES! How come you and I are the only ones who understand that about the *King Kong* remake?

GG: I don't know… it's all up there on the screen, if people watch with open minds.

CB: That's getting harder and harder for people to do.

GG: Thank goodness we're not affected by such cynicism.

CB: Getting back to *Billie*... Although Mike now realizes that he likes his new friend as a girl, Billie's awareness of feeling 'something special' won't occur until a few scenes from now. Instead of running races together, they'll be relating in a more romantic way. And then her great personal adventure really begins.

Girl Power

Reporter Ray Case and photographer Al Grant of *Life* magazine visit Harding High for "a little human interest story"... aka athletic wonder Billie Carol. Coach Ames calls her out of the practice line.

"Suppose you start by telling us how you learned to run so fast?" asks Case.

"Oh, that's easy. First of all I've been racing my dog, Clown, for years. I believe in competing with the best."

"I see."

"Then there's The Beat."

"The Beat?"

"Uh-huh. The Beat. You see, I hear it up here," Billie explains, pointing to her forehead. "And when I want to go faster, I speed up The Beat, and I go."

"You're putting me on!" smiles Case.

"No, really. You see track and field is like dance, without music," she amplifies. "And once you add the music, zoom, off you go!"

Billie demonstrates this with a little pole-vaulting... right into the arms and semi-battered body of her unfortunate father. Poor Howard shows up out of nowhere, freaks when he spots his airborne daughter, and catches her as she comes in for a landing. Both Carols land on the field, mussed and a bit flustered, but unharmed.

Is Coach Ames right about Mr. Carol being a nervous man without the old school spirit? Or is he just "a good father," as Billie maintains?

HOW DOES THE PRESS TREAT BILLIE?:

CB: First of all, let's give a big 'attagirl' to our heroine for keeping her composure and not letting the *Life* article go to her head. Others in her position wouldn't have handled sudden fame with as much grace and humility!

Sure, the only reason this national magazine sent reporters to do a human interest story was because the small town track-and-field phenom was a girl. But did they treat her with disrespect during the interview? Not at all! Did they ask her to do silly poses or goad her to be confrontational? No! They just presented Billie the way she is – and left it to America and the world to come to their own conclusions.

GG: Every 'first' comes at us by surprise, and given how desperately our culture needed intellectual upgrading in the early '60s, the inevitability of classifying an athletic female as an amusing oddity isn't at all surprising. You mean a girl actually beat a boy in a race? Heavens! What will they think of next? That said, Billie was covered by the reporters in a positive, non-condescending manner. With her fresh-faced charm and remarkable athletic talent, how could they not be impressed?

THE COACH'S MOTIVES

GG: Jones recognizes Billie's special skill instantly and pushes for its exploitation. He's thinking of glory for himself and his team, of course, especially if Harding's finest can be taught the mysterious Beat. But these selfish motives merely add color, even a little spice, to an old cliché (the valiant coach), and cranky-but-lovable was indeed actor Charles Lane's specialty. Jones is ultimately benign, even helpful to Billie's cause. And, as the next scene demonstrates, he has his funky, musical side.

A Different Beat?

Is The Beat transferable? Coach Ames' eyes light up at the prospect of Billie teaching her uncanny acceleration-through-music formula to the other members of his running team. For starters, she's successfully taught the Beat method to a few of her girlfriends. "Can they run?!" Ames asks. "No, they just like to dance."

Fair enough. The coach makes plans for a spirited workout later that night, the first Beat lesson for Harding's team. Billie asks if she can bring some of her girlfriends, and he agrees, adding that man-eating tigers would be welcome if it helps the cause.

"That's just about what some of them are," muses Billie.

At 8:00 in the Harding gym, a bongo-banging Coach Ames presides over Billie Carol's first class in How to Access The Beat and Speed Up Your Game. It's a musical romp as boys and girls respond to the rhythm, having a blast with every new dance step.

Mike's dancing on air as well... until he begins to notice that teacher Billie has quite a few students under her wing, including some very good-looking macho track stars.

Meanwhile, trouble of a very different kind is giving Howard Carol a headache. "Pull Billie off the track team," campaign manager Bullitt flatly advises, pointing out that their run for Mayoral office is running off the tracks.

"Aside from being ridiculous, it wouldn't be fair," Carol maintains, refusing the idea outright.

"To you or to her?"

"To either of us. And I don't want her hearing about it."

That would appear to be final, even for a politician.

HOW DOES BILLIE SOCIALLY INTERACT WITH WOMEN/GIRLFRIENDS?

GG: Billie has girlfriends, based on her dialogue with the coach and the people we see in the ensuing Beat number. But the pervasive melancholy and unique sensibilities of this misfit teen make imagining her joshing with boy-crazy girls a little hard to accept. That said, getting together once a week for an energetic dance class seems plausible. Being at ease with older sister Jeannie happily makes sense, and having a 'safe' boyfriend/fellow runner like Mike (Billie's surrogate sister, by her own Howard-like slip) also seems tomboy-appropriate. But in the final analysis, and for better or worse, disenfranchised Billie Carol seems most at home with the cute stuffed animal toys in her bedroom… a parallel she literally sings about.

CB: She has lots of female acquaintances, although her closest female friends appear to be her Mom and sister. Billie has been blessed by the example of a supportive mother and the unconditional love of a sister. And so she is more than open to cooperation rather than competition with others of her gender.

One of the most progressive, girl power inspiring elements of the movie is its lack of a ubiquitous 'mean girls' stereotypical sub-plot! Billie is shown as just one of the girls in the dance scene, accepted by the other females as an energetic 'mascot' type.

DANCE: AN ACCEPTABLE FORM OF FEMALE ATHLETICS?:

CB: Dance has been defined as "moving through space in time with intention," with 'movement' a showcase for technique, and 'intention' providing expression. In the dance scene, teen boys and girls are expressing the joy of having young healthy bodies that can move effortlessly and exuberantly! In 1965 there were cheerleading squads, but it would be a few years for dance and cheerleading to combine and evolve into forms like stepping, tall flags and dance drill teams. Each form has its own techniques and its unique intention… but at the end of the day, it's all dance.

GG: The idea of women dancing full-out (within reason), sometimes to the point of exhaustion, has been generally embraced by American society, as many of our nation's pioneers considered it, like tomboyism, to be welcome evidence of healthy breeding stock. The amazing physical moves in *Billie*'s dance numbers blow away anything we see the titular heroine accomplish in her tracksuit, with or without The Beat helping out. But dancing provides grace and elegant sweep designed to flow with music, providing dramatically feminine flourishes that registered as non-threatening to American males of the '60s.

POLITICAL CONSIDERATIONS VS. WHAT'S RIGHT:

CB: Despite political setbacks, Howard continues to demonstrate fair-mindedness, with concern for his daughter trumping campaign tactics. And am I the only one to catch the 'gender bender' aspect of his ever-present campaign button: CAROL FOR MAYOR. Just sayin'…

First Love

Beat lessons behind them, the kids relax at a local dance club. Billie enjoys some slow moves for a change, sharing a soft and soothing moment with partner Mike Benson.

"I've got a confession to make," he tells her. "I didn't like the idea of all those guys paying attention to you last night."

"Why?"

"I guess because I like you."

This is certainly nice to hear. "I like you too," says Billie. "And I'm glad we're friends."

"You are?"

"Mm-hm. You know, you're just about the best friend I've got."

Mike suddenly lights up inside.

"You're almost like my sister."

That earnest but unflattering comparison dims his glow. But only for a second. Mike's happy smile promptly returns; Billie is indeed the Billie for him.

Later that evening, the young runner/dancer/Beat instructor returns home. And waiting up for her is Agnes, who knows exactly what to make of her daughter's wistful eyes.

"Have a nice time?"

"We danced," Billie says softly. "Mike held my hand on the way home. I felt strange."

"In what way?"

"I dunno. Like… a girl."

Agnes smiles warmly and knowingly. "You'll find being a girl is an easy adjustment to make."

"I like it," Billie whispers happily.

A short while later in her room, Billie revisits familiar thoughts… which now have a new spin.

I must be growing up
I'd like to run and hide
There's something going on
I'm all mixed up inside

Tonight he held my hand,
And when our fingers touched
I felt butterflies
Funny little butterflies…

I wonder if it shows
This strange new way I feel
This strange new feeling
That I simply can't conceal

Tonight, he held me tight
And all the while we danced
I felt butterflies
Funny little butterflies…

I'm still a little scared…
It happens much too fast
I'm still a little lost
Between what's coming
And what's past

I know it's not a dream
It's lasted much too long
Each time I close my eyes
The feelings still so strong

Tonight, I found it nice
Just to be a girl
I feel butterflies
Funny little butterflies inside

A whole new world has just opened up for Billie Carol... challenging, a little scary, but, oh, so wonderful!

WHAT A MOM SHOULD DO AND SAY:

CB: Heaven protect us from the notion that a daughter only learns from what her mother *says* to her!

Daughters learn every day from their mothers by watching what they do and how they act in addition to what they say. Agnes Carol is a complex woman who shows that being a stay-at-home mom does not automatically turn one into a mindless drone. An intelligent, witty woman, she is physically attractive and still very much an object of desire for her husband of over twenty years. Furthermore, one can easily infer from her with Howard about their courtship that she was somewhat innocent when he, the upperclassman, came in and swept her off her feet. There's more than a bit of innuendo to suggest that Howard wooed and won the lovely Agnes due in part to his very dominant sexuality.

Therefore, when Agnes tells her daughter "You'll find being a girl is an easy adjustment to make," maybe she's telling Billie that it's easy to follow your heart. The adjustment isn't one that forces a girl to sacrifice her ambitions or 'dumb down' her personality. It's the adjustment that allows a girl to follow her heart behind a closed bedroom door – where she will find delight in the joys of submission to her alpha male.

GG: Right.

Most of what Agnes Carol says is generally rock solid common sense, so it's tempting to measure every word or line reading for signs of negative social conditioning. Here's a sly one: "You'll find being a girl is an easy adjustment to make," which unconsciously suggests that blissful non-challenging pleasures await the savvy female who trades 'manly' pursuits of individual achievement (tomboyism/proto-feminism) in favor of placid servitude, the miracle of motherhood, and, quite possibly, genuine love and affection from a provider-husband. Is it more satisfying to be 'kept' super-comfortably, or to struggle a little and push personal potential to the max, maybe changing the world in the process? Housewife Agnes has clearly made up her mind what the proper choice should be, or perhaps she's smart enough to allow her more socially-advanced daughter to experiment with different personal options. But an extra line about "not forgetting who you are even as you're losing your head over first love" would have been solid advice from a responsible mom, especially considering what happens next.

IS IT REALLY LOVE?

GG: I buy it. Actors Duke and Berlinger have personal chemistry, and the fact that he's considerably older than his diminutive co-star gives Mike's consciousness-raising lessons from Billie additional bite. As suggested earlier, a cute, smart tomboy may be just right for semi-shy Benson, and they are clearly kindred spirits on the sports field and off.

CB: Yes! It is indeed love. And for Billie, it is first love. Sigh…

The Girl is a Girl is a Girl

Mike, perfecting his Beat technique, is getting a little private tutoring from Billie, which prompts some good-natured ribbing from his teammates in the locker room. "It's all for one and one for all… and we know which one," the guys laugh, whooping it up. But hey, who can resist the inexhaustible charms of the remarkable lady in question? Or any female of the species, for that matter?

The girl is a girl is a girl
In her jeans or fancy clothes
The girl is a girl is a girl
And we like the way it shows
She's a female wonder who steals our thunder
She's way out front in all our sports
But who can complain
When she looks so terrific in shorts?

A girl is a girl is a girl
In a sweatshirt or a gown
A girl is a girl is a girl
And so great to have around
Though we can't out-race her
We love to chase her
She leaves a trail of sweet perfume
A girl is a girl is a girl
Even in a locker room

We help her zip her zippers
We leave the mirror free
She walks around in curlers

Just as cute as she could be
We have to watch our language
We try to be polite
We see her every morning
And we'd like to every night

The girl is a girl is a girl
And she makes it understood
The girl is a girl is a girl
And she makes the team look good
She's a plan in action, the main attraction
She makes a lady to a 'T'
A girl is a girl is a girl
And we all agree
A girl is a girl is a girl
And she's all a girl should be!

ATTITUDE OF THE GUYS TOWARD BILLIE:

CB: The admirable way that the young men on the team embrace Billie is just an example of the inherent decency of young men. Maybe they patronize her a bit, maybe they treat her like a 'kid sister' or even a team mascot, but these are totally appropriate interactions, given the way she acts and looks.

GG: Her impressed male athletic colleagues seem to regard tomboyish Billie with big-brotherly fondness, although she's girlish enough to inspire a few candy-coated salacious remarks in the locker room. Essentially BC's a patronized mascot, an oddity on a parallel track with their ambitions, but never a genuine threat to ego.

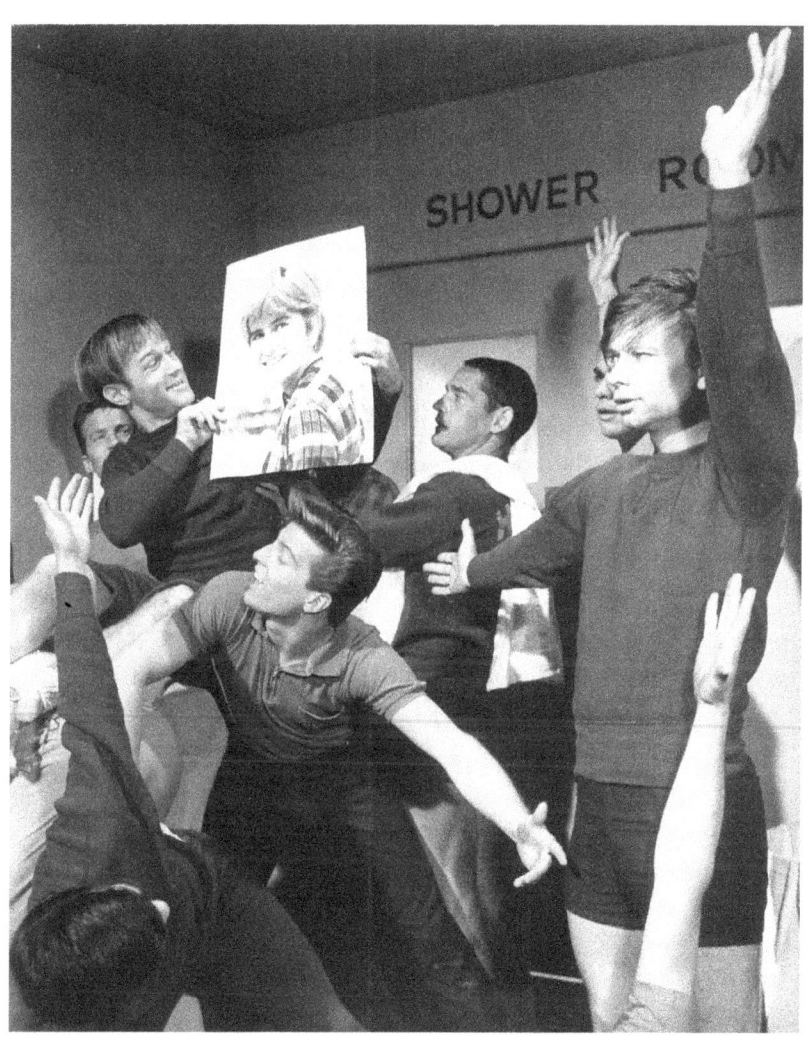

ATTITUDE OF THE GUYS TOWARD WOMEN IN GENERAL:

GG: The locker room production number, sort of *Billie*'s low-budget answer to "There Ain't Nothing Like a Dame" (*South Pacific*), has become a highlight of the film for camp-craving gay audiences, who delight in watching muscular-yet-graceful dancer/athletes prancing about in a song that requires them to mock female behavior and gestures. With a girl behaving like a boy and a bunch of energetic jocks imitating females, *Billie*'s eventual reputation as a gender-bending curio really can't be questioned.

CB: As a young girl watching this locker room musical number my reaction was pure, unadulterated bliss (it was the teen version of a similar number from *Damn Yankees!*, "You Gotta Have Heart")! Okay, so as an adult I can't help but realize that this scene might be equally as fun to watch for gay men, but I didn't really know what 'gay' was back then. All I knew was there were a bunch of really cute boys in various stages of undress who were singing and dancing in celebration of my heroine Billie Carol! Yay!

Curiously, watching as an adult I couldn't help but imagine how cool it would've been to have Billy De Wolfe join the fun with a cameo appearance by his tipsy, cross-dressing alter-ego Mrs. Murgatroid? Perhaps as Mrs. Murgatroid playing Eddie's mom, Mrs. Davis? Hmmm…

GG: The skeleton in Mayor Davis' closet. No wonder poor Eddie turned out the way he did…

CB: Speaking of Eddie, he was the captain of the track team, but he was *never* the alpha male. If he had been, he would've been surrounded by a posse of sycophants when he first teased Billie at the beginning of the movie. The other guys were too smart for that.

Also, this once arch-enemy of Billie seems to become a patronizing admirer mid-way through the film, no different from his teammates. I believe he's even one of the two jocks who happily carries her about in that impromptu school parade.

Romance vs. Equal Rights

Has Billie been tamed by the love bug? Is she throwing race after race just to have her almost-boyfriend Mike Benson, who just happens to be the competition, feel like a winner?

"Carol! Don't you feel well?" shouts a horrified Coach Ames. "You finished second to Mike in every event! You've lost The Beat! And our first meet's Saturday!"

"I'll be there," Billie answers blissfully, still under the magical spell of first love.

Ah, what a wonderful feeling. But it doesn't take long before certain realities hit home… especially since young Mr. Benson is not at all happy about the guys making fun of his relationship with their resident Beat instructor. He and Billie get together on the school grounds.

"Boy, you were great today!" compliments Billie.

"Thanks," responds Mike with little enthusiasm.

"Something wrong?"

"Billie, I've got to talk to you."

"About what?"

"About us."

"Oh. Okay. Go ahead."

"I've decided you've got to do something," Mike proclaims, "because everybody's making jokes and laughing at me."

"You want me to hit them?" the tomboy asks innocently.

"No… I've decided that you should not only give up the track team, you've got to stop dancing with other boys."

Wow. Billie's more than a little taken aback by Mike's no-nonsense order.

"That's what you've decided," she states, almost to convince herself of what's just been said.

"That's right."

"I see. In other words, you don't believe in equality, like my father."

"Well sure I believe in equality. But I think you should compete as a girl, not as a boy."

"Well if everybody's equal, what difference does it make how I compete?"

"It makes a difference, because men and women are equal, but not the same. If there wasn't any difference I'd go out on a date with Eddie Davis!"

"What for? I can run faster than he can."

"Billie, that's *not* why I like you!"

This opens up an interesting question. She looks Mike straight in the eye. "Why *do* you like me?"

"Because you're a girl."

"And that's why you don't want me to compete against men?"

"Yes!"

"Then you don't think of me as an equal."

"Well sure I do. But I think of you as a girl first."

"Well I want you to think of me as an equal first."

This exchange seems to be going nowhere. Flustered, Mike stands, shakes his head at the whole offbeat conversation. "Oh go ahead, do want you want," he whines. "I don't want to talk about it."

But in her own low-key way, Billie is relentless. "You don't want to talk about it because you know you're wrong," she retorts.

"I'm *not* wrong!"

"Okay. You'll find out tomorrow when I run you into the ground!"

With that, Billie takes off. An equally upset Mike gives chase, but his tomboy semi-girlfriend isn't pulling punches this time. She's making full use of The Beat and hauling ass like a comet – so he hasn't a chance of catching up.

WHAT SHE GIVES UP FOR LOVE:

GG: Throwing a race and letting the man feel superior when she can easily defeat her opponent is the last thing Billie Carol would do… normally. Unprepared by even a relatively progressive mom for the seductive down side of romantic love and the importance of self-integrity, Billie goes through hell trying to figure all this basic stuff out for herself. While every teenager in any era must endure her rites of passage, at least today's enlightened parents aren't afraid to share some pretty obvious and not so pretty truths with their kids.

CB: Let's be clear about something: Billie never intentionally 'throws' the race to Mike! She stands on the starting line, ready to race, and we watch as she tries to summon The Beat. What happens next is obvious to anyone who remembers what it felt like to be in love for the very first time. Billie is unable to 'hear' The Beat over the beating of her own heart.

Remember those feelings – the heady mix of sweetness and sensuality, romance and lust – all mixed up in the crucible of the adolescent heart? If you have any doubt about it, just look at Billie's expression as she literally looks up at Mike. Billie in love is a girl without The Beat, and without that she cannot win the face.

GG: At no time does Billie have trouble accessing The Beat... the energizing music in her head would be presented as garbled all of a sudden, and we'd be getting dialogue like, "What's wrong with me? I've lost The Beat!" followed by an all-wise Mom saying "Don't you know why? The love bug has bitten you. You're a grown-up girl now." And, as we know, grown-up girls promptly put childhood frivolity behind them, including record-shattering athletics. It's the old parable of the virgin and the unicorn, designed to show how precious female skills and interests MUST evaporate with the coming of adulthood, and when measured against the love of a man.

By the way, Billie, in total control other than being under the influence of first love, *deliberately* holds herself back at the starting line for a few pivotal seconds before blasting off, something Coach Ames witnesses. Billie hasn't lost her unique athletic skills; she's simply not accessing them so that the boy she loves can come out a winner. Fortunately, she realizes how foolish this is before the 'big event'.

BILLIE SOLVES PROBLEMS BY HITTING PEOPLE?

CB: Mike is starting to flex his boyfriend muscles, so to speak, and this conversation allows us to discover that he isn't quite there as an alpha male. When Billie asks Mike "Do you want me to hit them?" she's reverting to safer 'tomboy' mode.

GG: 'Hitting bullies' is a tomboy trope, like 'climbing trees' and 'playing baseball'. Spunky heroine Billie Carol does none of these things, but as she was designed to be the ultimate hoyden icon fleshed out by an actress, the words fit into Patty Duke's mouth sociologically, just not realistically. The smart, patient, mad-only-when-pushed-too-far young idealist we've bonded with would never use her fists to settle an argument, except maybe as a last resort, or perhaps when she was a pre-teen. Billie's other efforts to sound tomboy-tough don't exactly work either, probably because they seem too primal and childish, at total odds with the clear-thinking intellectual who has so impressed us.

CAN BOTH BE RIGHT?

GG: Telling Billie that he likes her 'because she's a girl' rather than an individual he's come to care for may be more a confusion of terms. What Mike's really trying to say is that he cares for Billie romantically, more than just the way he feels about a friend – sex be damned. Points for Mike. Even so, Billie rightfully needs to assert her individuality and ascertain equal status before considering the plusses and risks of first romance, much as she seems to crave it.

CB: When it comes to the heart, there is no 'right' or 'wrong' – the heart wants what the heart wants! So in their discussion, we see the problem Mike is having as he engages in a 'debate' with Billie because he's talking about how he *feels* while she's telling him what she *thinks*. The really, really significant thing that happens during this exchange is we see Billie finally finding her inner brat, proving that the sexual tension is starting to bubble up to the surface for our heroine. Throwing down her version of the "Anything You Can Do (I Can Do Better)" challenge, our feisty girl-on-the-brink is adorable as she hoydens up and threatens to run Mike "into the ground" at the upcoming track meet.

PATTY DUKE AS "BILLIE"

Phenom or Albatross?

Poor Howard. He's overwhelmed by the national publicity generated by *Life*'s coverage, with his 'Women Shouldn't Compete with Men' speech a coast-to-coast howler. It looks like his mayoral campaign is a total bust.

"When Billie comes home we'll simply explain the situation to her," offers a sympathetic Agnes.

"I wouldn't dream of suppressing that child," Howard stubbornly proclaims. "Tonight I'm going to debate Mayor Davis for the second time. I can hardly wait to be regarded as a national laughing shrine. Oh, why couldn't she have been a boy…"

Almost on cue, Billie bursts into the house, still enraged by her argument with Mike. "I think all men *stink*!"

Howard takes this in stride. "Don't retract that statement because I'm here."

"I wasn't going to!"

Billie runs up the stairs, to her room. "That's the child you want me to reason with," Howard tells Agnes with a shake of the head. "I couldn't get her off that team with a whip."

That evening at the town hall debate, Mayor Davis continues his innuendo-laden smear campaign. "There are goings on in the Carol home that are both un-Christian and un-American," he announces with grim concern, tantalizing a fair but gossip-friendly audience. Full disclosure of these 'goings on' will come during or before the final mayoral debate, Davis promises.

"Nobody can believe that a fifteen-year-old girl running on a boys' track team is either un-Christian or un-American," disgruntled Howard gripes to Agnes later that night. The unexpected arrival of Bob Mathews couldn't be more ironic. Much to Bob's palpable frustration, Jeannie insists on keeping their marriage secret… a move that gets even more dicey when she goes out on a Dad-encouraged date with Matt Bullitt!

As for in-the-know Billie, she's "jumping for joy," which dovetails perfectly with her relentless hurdle practice about the family sofa. "I want to be in the best condition of my life tomorrow," she proclaims with heartfelt determination. "I'll show Mike…"

DISSING DAD, ETC.:

CB: Voila! Ladies and Gentlemen, introducing the mood swings, rebelliousness, bad manners, self-absorption and general malaise that's known as adolescence. We need no further proof beyond this classic outburst that our heroine has gone 'from bobby socks to stockings' and that Billie is officially a 'teenager in love'.

GG: Precisely. It's interesting what this outburst tells us about Billie, and her personality swings. One minute we're impressed with the most rational and well-mannered young person imaginable, the next we're ducking for cover as a mini-volcano explodes. This is more Patty Duke channeling her own troubled psyche than relatively consistent Ginger Carol by Ronald Alexander, or rather a deeper characterization that developed when the actress who played Helen Keller sunk her first-class teeth into the part.

'UN-CHRISTIAN AND UN-AMERICAN':

GG: The closest we'll get to direct social/political satire in *Billie*. A crass politician using sacred cows for campaign propaganda mostly reminds viewers of the hypocrisy of all parties involved. Generally speaking, a socially-enlightened modern family would have avoided most of this film's plot contrivances simply by being more mature, intelligent, and honest about their feelings and problems.

CB: Mayor Davis certainly thinks he's Ken Star holding the Gap dress, doesn't he? The really sad thing in all this, in my opinion, is that his smarmy plan to 'out' Jeannie as an unwed mother probably would've worked for that audience. Bob hadn't made an honest woman of her.

BILLIE'S DETERMINATION:

CB: Billie is now running in the footsteps of brats since time immemorial! Just like Kate tested Petrucchio, so our Billie is now testing Mike. Her pride tells her to "run him into the ground." Her mind tells her to "run him into the ground."

But what about her heart? She doesn't think about it consciously, but her submissive heart is telling her that what she really wants is to run her fastest race… and come in second to her alpha male.

(This is the juncture in their relationship where all the good little subs in the audience hold their breath and pray: please Mike, don't let her get away with that! In their fantasies, he takes her by the shoulders, firmly but calmly, and stands a bit too close, forcing her to literally look up – way up – as he scolds her. "Billie, that's enough! Just because I'm a gentleman doesn't mean I won't turn you over my knee!" Anyone who's read a blog dedicated to 'missed spanking opportunities in movies' knows that *Billie* is exactly the type of movie that is deliciously ripe for such naughty conjecture!)

GG: Spanking Billie? What a concept! But I'd trust nice-guy Mike, who's been on the receiving end of her temper lately and would probably enjoy turning things around. If Howard Carol is right about women, the Beat Wonder herself would probably benefit from a harmless paddling, being put 'in her place' and all. As a matter of fact, both Billie and Mike, experimental and physically-oriented types, probably have a charming fetish future ahead of them, if that's what floats their boat.

But even so… Lightning-fast emotionally as well as on the sports field, lovestruck Billie suddenly devolves from total tomboy to hapless, dreamy-eyed teen girl. Instead of using The Beat to beat boys, she now finishes behind Her Man in every race because she loves him so… and, let's face it, the poor sap can use all the help he can get. Finally, after a socially-relevant spat with Mike that rightfully outrages Billie, she pulls a fierce 180 and threatens to demolish him athletically. High time.

The Beat Beats All!

It's morning at Harding High, and the bleachers are filled with cheering locals. The decathlon, greatest of all school-related athletic events, is about to commence.

"Take your marks," the tracksuited runners are told after these impressive contenders limber up at the start line. Billie is among them, and she shoots a challenging look at competitor Mike. Then she positions herself.

"Get ready…"

Billie summons The Beat. She bobs her head as the inner rhythm gains momentum, smiles as her eyes sparkle with growing confidence…

Bang! And the runners are off!

Focused and on her game, Billie swiftly rockets ahead of the boys. Spectators in the bleachers roar their approval! And cheering loudest is mayoral candidate/proudest of dads Howard Carol, along with the rest of the Carol family.

A force of female nature with no self-imposed restrictions this time, Billie fulfills her promise from yesterday's rant: she runs poor Mike Benson into the ground. That's along with each and every one of her sturdy male competitors, including iron-pumping super specimen Eddie Davis. All of these guys were just taught The Beat by Billie, and it certainly shows in their improved athletic performance. But Billie is clearly master of this unique technique… and she's really pouring it on this morning, in one remarkable demonstration of strength and stamina after another.

Patty Duke as "Billie"

The Story

Hurdles? No trouble for Billie, who clears every one in the blink of an eye.

Javelins? Young Billie hauls back and throws one mightily, as the crowd cheers.

And what about Daddy's personal favorite, pole-vaulting? With every Beat-invigorated muscle rising to the formidable challenge, Billie races forward, plants her pole and gracefully careens over the highly-set bar. YES! More deafening applause.

Speaking of Daddy, Howard and the entire Carol clan cheer happily from the stands, aglow with pride every time Billie does something spectacular. Which is more often than not, much to the chagrin of another interested spectator with an offspring in the field, Mayor Davis.

Indeed, young Miss Carol has never felt The Beat so strongly. All of last night's couch-jumping exercises, heightened by personal anger, seem to be serving her extremely well this morning. Every emotion shows on the

The Story

athlete's face – supreme confidence, exceptional concentration, concern about properly timing her interaction with teammates – the earmarks of a true champion.

Only in the final contest does Billie appear to lose a little ground, and it's clearly not her fault. Luckless Mike screws up in the Baton Pass, costing his partner BC a few precious moments. Has this mishap broken her momentum?

No-no-no and a half! The Beat Maiden of Harding High automatically warps into emergency drive, summoning inner reserves of power that she's never required before, or even suspected she had!

...and The Beat brings it all home! A jubilant Billie Carol whips past her opponents and wins this final racing contest. What an unprecedented decathlon performance!

Everyone's caught in mid-cheer as an announcement comes over the loudspeaker...

"Ladies and gentlemen... Miss Billie Carol is awarded the honor of Athlete of the Day."

Which pretty much says it all. As cheering spectators and proud family members watch, weeping-for-joy Billie is hoisted upon the shoulders of her male competitors and carried off, the shining star of an impromptu parade.

It's quite a scene. Everyone sings this super-girl's praises – literally – with Mike, recovering from his less-than-stellar performance, honestly happy about her triumph. And one of those two boys carrying Billie is none other than formerly obnoxious Eddie Davis, now won over by his teammate's spirit and undeniable athletic prowess. Maybe his Dad, the mayor, likes to play dirty, but Eddie recognizes quality in a competitor when he sees it (*and* gets clobbered by it).

And talk about a proud father! Howard is so thrilled by Billie's remarkable exploits that he briefly forgets about his nagging political concerns, sure to reach a climax in tonight's big debate.

"There's my little star!" he says lovingly as the family gathers in Billie's makeshift locker room. "Five-foot-two and a half inches of greased lightning. You were great today, son!"

Groan. Agnes and Jeannie exchange embarrassed looks. And Billie manages her familiar sad smile, accompanied by a shrug.

IS BILLIE'S PERFORMANCE CREDIBLE?

GG: Patty Duke is the first to admit that she was never an athlete. She's short and stocky and nothing like the long-limbed, ultra-sleek and muscular female runners who compete in professional contests. Cherubic Billie probably needs a funky super-power like The Beat to outperform genuine

racers, male or female. Once again, three cheers for Duke's fine acting, which makes her somewhat ungainly speed demon heroine fully convincing.

CB: Hip, hip, and hooray! Three cheers for Patty Duke as Billie! She is small but mighty! Five feet two and a half inches of girl power – inspiring dynamite!

IS THE PARADE CONDESCENDSING/WHY EXACTLY IS BILLIE WEEPING?

CB: The Victory Parade literally shows our heroine being raised up 'above' the other members of the team. If this had happened before she met Mike, fell in love and moved onto the 'adolescent' phase of her life, Billie would have been crying tears of joy. Indeed, she would have been thrilled to please her father and delight her mother and sister, while basking in the admiration of her coach and teammates. Yes, *tomboy* Billie, as the victorious 'Athlete of the Day', would've been in heaven!

Look closely at Billie's face – are those tears of joy? Absolutely not! That's because tomboy Billie is gone, and gone forever. In her new role as a brat she's carried out her threat and ran Mike "into the ground." So why is she broken-hearted? Because more than anything she wanted to come in second to him! More than anything she wanted to cheer him on as the team lifted *him* aloft.

Logical? Nope. True? Oh, hell yes its true! The shrew wants to be tamed as much as her man wants to tame her – and there is no happy ending until this occurs. In *Annie Get Your Gun* the heroine sabotages her own rifle to make sure she comes in second, a valid choice when love trumps foolish pride!

Both Billie and Mike are finding their sea legs on the rocky ship of romance, so they both have to endure this stormy event. But there's hope, because Billie is strong enough to feel her feelings and have a good cry. Mike, to his credit, handles the situation magnificently, once again proving he is a good sport, a good friend and a worthy object of our heroine's affection.

GG: Yes and no. On the one hand it's a spontaneous outpouring of genuine positive emotion, on the other it's mid-'60s chauvinism unconsciously reducing an accomplished female athlete to a cute novelty, a 'curio' as Ginger once put it in a different incarnation.

It's logical to assume Billie's tears are joyful… she's won, proven her point to Mike, and everyone is now (literally) looking up to her. But given the sustained melancholy of the character and those pertinent social issues that *Billie* half-consciously explores, it's reasonable to read this tearful response as an overall comment about a still complacent, still sexist culture that requires far more advancement before it's capable of truly 'getting it'.

HOWARD'S GOOF: THE BOY THING AGAIN:

GG: Actually, given how hard Billie has worked to be the boy her Dad always wanted, the fact that Howard happily responds to her as one by mistake shouldn't be that unexpected, shocking or traumatic. If Billie had told him earlier that "Okay, I'm female, but I can do everything the boy you really wanted can," that would be one thing. But she simply tells her Dad "I wish I was a boy," and he agrees.

No one denies that this final goofy slip is an embarrassing moment for Howard Carol, but is it also a case of Billie feeling the heat for embarking on a political agenda that makes her a freedom-seeking, but ultimately sexless, equal? No one is letting asleep-at-the-wheel conservative Howard off the hook for being part of a culture that set this mess in motion, but Billie has to learn that every great crusade requires sacrifice. If you want to be a boy so badly but bristle at the down side of genderless acceptance, well, watch out what you wish for, Billie Carol… and be prepared for a little more heartache.

CB: Billie is already hurting because she feels uncomfortable beating Mike – but the insult is added to injury when her father calls her 'son'. No longer feeling like a child, she no longer wants to act like a boy. Sadly, her Dad is clueless at this point in the story. And, to be fair, his faux pas was thoughtless. So right now, Billie feels rejected as a girl… by both Mike and her Dad. Talk about teenage angst!

What a Woman Wants

Is Howard Carol "The most understanding and tolerant man in the world?" This exasperated self-assessment is put to the test when he and his family return from Harding High. It's guileless Billie who joyously jumps the gun with some startling personal news – "Bob and Jeannie are going to have a baby!" This prompts an understandably enraged Howard to punch poor Bob first, ask for his new son-in-law's forgiveness – and mayoral endorsement – later.

"Good Christian man" Charlie Davis gets this bombshell news right between his beady eyes during that evening's town debate, bringing the mayor's creepy smear campaign to a merciful end. Not only are Bob and Jeannie Matthews married, but Bob's about to become Howard's new law partner – black eye and all.

And so Harding elects itself a new mayor. But is Howard Carol truly "the most understanding and tolerant man in the world"? He gets a chance to prove it when a despondent Billie asks him to be her date for his victory dinner. "I feel kind of funny, and unhappy," she tells Howard, who reassures her that all kids go through this kind of emotional confusion at her age. "It's a little thing called growing pains," he explains.

In any event, athletic wonder Billie Carol wants to dress up and have a date this evening, so a pleased Howard complies. That's just before the real person Billie wants to date shows up at their front door. Determined Mike Benson explains to Howard that he and she recently had a fight – he demanded that she quit the track team, she suggested he take a walk. So now Mike's hoping to ask Billie out on a date in a reasonable and logic move to get back in her good graces.

Still, "In dealing with women, a man must shun reason and logic," Howard pithily explains, offering some advice from his own, rich personal experience. "Time has shown that the male of the species has never been able to turn these two weapons to his advantage." The answer? "Confusion," Howard suggests, although he readily admits that this strategy might not work on Billie. "Action and dedication," he states emphatically. "A woman of fifteen is impressed with shining knights and holy grails. At sixteen they smile indulgently at growing boys, and when she reaches my wife's age she laughs openly." What does this all amount to? "You can't ask Billie to that dance. You've got to tell her she's going with you."

"Heh. She'd kill me."

"No, you've got to be strong and dominant, and in doing so you've got to let her know that no matter what she does or is, she's still your girl."

Mike respectfully disagrees. "Billie and I have never had to resort to intrigue," he proclaims with unrestrained pride. "Our relationship has been much more mature than that."

Howard shrugs. "All right, you're the victim. I'll call her and tell her. I'll be on the porch listening, in case you have a few last words for posterity."

HOWARD'S VIEW:

CB: The groundwork has been laid in an earlier scene to indicate that Howard, at Mike's age, was a dynamic and aggressive suitor. He tells Agnes he was 'mature' during their courtship, but she says with unabashedly sexual overtones that he was 'advanced'. And then she practically purrs, saying that at seventeen she was so glad he took the lead. (Just in case there's any doubt that they are a sexually active couple, we discover that Agnes is pregnant!)

Howard knew how to woo and win Agnes, and he knows what Mike needs to do to win Billie. A smaller person wouldn't help Mike, but Howard

Carol is not a small person! Howard Carol is an alpha male who passes the baton, so to speak, to his future son-in-law. Strong-willed women are usually sexually attracted to dominant men – and the Carol women truly are nothing if not strong-willed!

Howard clearly tells Mike to live and let live when it comes to the decisions of everyday life – after all, Howard and Agnes aren't a 'Taken in Hand' 24/7 HoH couple! But Howard sees that Mike is faltering in his resolve, so he steps in to coach and share his uniquely masculine strategies. Howard lets his 'alpha apprentice' know that his daughter doesn't need 'reason and logic'. Like her mother before her, Billie needs to know that when it comes to romance, it's okay to submit to your alpha male. No, not only okay – it is absolutely necessary for both parties!

GG: Cutting to the chase: It's that ancient conservative argument that the strongest heterosexual feminist leader will always succumb to and be tamed by the strongest alpha male. Strong-willed women need to be dominated by primal, non-intellectual, father-like males if they wish to achieve total visceral and sexual satisfaction – the body doesn't lie, after all. Paging Russell Crowe.

Howard's advice to Mike mirrors Clarence Day's romantic advice to his befuddled son: "Be firm!" Even 1949 audiences may have caught the secondary meaning of this. But the "let them rant, then lay down the law with forcefulness and they'll worship you for it" approach to handling women is still pretty much standard practice among modern alphas. Some women love it. Others are horrified by it. The majority seem to want it at bedtime, as a fantasy, but 'revert' to untamed, equal-if-not-better status at every other hour of the day.

MIKE'S VIEW:

CB: Howard sees a lot of himself in Mike – and being a confident man, he likes what he sees! His decision to mentor Mike is just another example of male bonding – the way that genuinely admirable men support each other. As he mentors Mike, we see that Howard has realized that his little girl has grown up, and the time to treat Billie as either a boy or a child is past.

So when Mike explains his 'logic and reason' strategy to win Billie's heart, Howard decides to pass the 'alpha baton' to this worthy young gentleman. Of all his accomplishments – successful attorney, mayor-elect of Harding, USA among them –Howard is most proud of his rock solid marriage to a woman that many had thought 'out of his league'. He imparts the secrets of being dominant "at least 40% of the time" to the skeptical Mike.

Mike shows us that he respects Billie as an equal, just as she had hoped. But when he hears Howard extolling the virtues of bold action, it strikes a chord in Mike's alpha-in-training soul. The moment when Mike realizes that Billie's father *wants* him to be dominant with his daughter his world view starts to shift. (Maybe those thoughts he's had late at night – pulling the girl across his knee, lifting that short skirt up to reveal white cotton panties… this is for her own good…)

GG: It's hard for a guy to argue with this kind of logic. But I'll give it a shot…

Mike tries to be a progressive thinker by declaring that he and Billie have an honest relationship, and that resorting to macho tactics, even carefully measured ones, wouldn't fool such an intelligent girl. *Billie* naturally proves him wrong in the next scene, reminding us that the true purpose of Alexander's scenario is for complacent Americans to pat themselves on the back for those fine old-fashioned conservative values… ironically enough, a philosophy that harkens back to his original sexist speech at Harding High.

By the way, Case, are you free this Friday night? I'll bring the paddle.

CB: I'll let you know.

An Equal and a Girlfriend

Softly feminine in a pink dress, Billie is stunned and slightly irked at the presence of former boyfriend Mike (or is it just 'boy friend'?) waiting for her downstairs.

"Hi Billie."

"What do you want?"

"Well, I came to ask you to the dance tonight."

"You did? Well, *no*, thank you."

"Why not?!"

"Because you're just like every other man, Mike. You're not big enough in character to accept me as a real equal."

"Billie, this is not the time to be emotional –"

"Don't interrupt! It's all your fault I'm not accepted as a girl."

"*My* fault?!"

"That's right. If you hadn't been so petty and narrow-minded you'd have taken me out and said to everybody 'This is my girl.'"

"Yes, my girl, the *track star*…"

"Why not?"

"Because people laugh."

"And you're afraid they're laughing at you. Mike, you're a coward!"

"That's not true."

"Yes, it is. You're passive instead of active and I don't want to see you again."

So much for reason. There's nothing left to do except follow some of Howard Carol's questionable advice. Gritting his teeth, Mike takes the inevitable plunge. "Now, hold it!" he demands in an uncharacteristically loud voice.

Which stops Billie in her high-heeled tracks. "Are you talking to me?"

"That's right. Have you finished what you have to say?"

"Just about."

"Good, because I have something to tell you."

"Go ahead."

"You were right, and I was wrong," Mike sighs, combining new-found courage with his customary compassion. "As far as I'm concerned, you can do whatever you want. You're not my equal. You're my better. Good night." And with that, he walks away.

"Hold it!" Billie shouts. Then she walks right over to him with a no-nonsense expression, and Mike isn't sure what the feisty fifteen-year-old has in mind. "Listen, you… Aren't you gonna ask me to go to the dance?"

"I *did* ask you."

"Would you ask me again?"

"All right. Do you wanna go to the dance with me tonight?"

"Sure. Let's go."

Mike beams. "Don't you think we ought to tell your mother and father?"

"Nah. They'll never miss me."

"Just a minute," Howard's voice rings out from the porch.

Billie is stunned. "Daddy, I didn't know you were out there!"

"Obviously."

BILLIE'S NEED TO GIRL-UP:

CB: Billie as tomboy never balks at wearing dresses – but she looks childish in the dress she wore to the debate, with its oversized bow and unflattering shape. When she changes to go to Victory Party, she is following up on her heartwarming talk with her Daddy. Sitting on his lap, Billie asked if she could be his 'date' for the evening. (This reminds me of the creepy 'Father/Daughter Chastity Ball' events that are all the vogue these days among many of the 'Just Say No' Christian right.)

When she descends the staircase with her smart hairdo and stylish empire-waist cocktail dress, she is a teenage vision of loveliness and totally 1965 red carpet ready! This is the 'big reveal', echoing the moment when Calamity Jane takes off her army coat and voila, she's a dazzling young woman in a pretty party dress! No one talked Billie into this new look – this is her choice!

She's unsure of many things, but one thing is clear – she wants to grow up and be not just a girl but a girlfriend. Having a beautiful and stylish mother and older sister helps make her transition from the awkward dresses of youth to the 'belle of the ball' ensembles a lot easier. (Most of the tween girls in the audience were big fans of *The Patty Duke Show* and we thought, "Oh – that's a real 'Cathy' look!"). What resonates in this scene is the fact that dressing up in party clothes, and the admiration that this brings, can make any girl feel like a princess.

GG: Billie's dressing up appropriately (read: femininely) for the Mayor-elect's victory party seems logical enough. This young woman knows when to challenge the status quo and when to enjoy its pleasing benefits. The combination of her own special athletic triumph and her Dad's winning of the election entitles Billie to enter the town hall justified, head held high, and happy as the proverbial lark.

Of course, every father has a right to say "awwww" when his tomboy daughter puts on that pretty party dress for the first time and pretends she's a

princess going to a ball. It's both cruel and unfair to trivialize the feelings of trepidation a girl experiences as she faces the judgment of peers and parents in this kind of social petri dish.

But the inevitable question comes to mind, reminding me of Garbo's famous statement after watching Cocteau's *Beauty and the Beast*... What has become of that wonderful, natural creature Belle and the audience fell in love with? As a fast-lane tomboy, Billie was special, memorable, and seemed completely comfortable in innocently sexy athletic gear. As a conventional American princess, she appears ungainly, unremarkable and to many, a little butch. Mike doesn't know it yet, but he'll eventually want girlfriend Billie to put on the sexy running shorts and sweatshirt again, because they better represent the individual that he fell in love with.

HOW MIKE HANDLES BILLIE:

CB: *"Hold it!"*

His deep voice booming, we hear those two words and know that Mike Benson has just lets his alpha male flag fly! We see Billie react instinctively, stopping short and giving Mike her undivided attention. As her father predicted, she responds favorably to Mike's show of strength as he proves he will fight for her love.

Just as Billie's inner transformation from tomboy to teenager in love was symbolized by her party dress reveal, so too is Mike's transformation from friend to boyfriend symbolized by this new 'take-charge' attitude and deep baritone voice. Calm but commanding, firm but fair, he shows Billie he is ready, willing and able to be a man that she can respect, and be proud of being 'his girl'.

Once Mike has established himself as the dominant in their relationship, he does something wonderful – he admits that he was wrong about the way he handled the athletic competition between them. Boldly, he looks her squarely in the eyes and says forcefully: "You're not my equal. You're my better."

Mike acknowledges her superior prowess on the track field because he finally understands that the track field is one isolated part of their lives – and that he doesn't need to physically dominate Billie in sports to be dominant romantically.

Billie finds this new Mike completely irresistible – a forceful man (like her beloved Daddy) who understands her 'Equals First' philosophy. She uses his line, "Hold it!" for a really cute turn-about-is-fair-play exchange. Billie is now 'playing' the dominant part in order to show him her playful submissive side. Coy and adorable, she asks Mike to ask her to the Victory Dance. A true gentleman, he graciously accepts her gesture and their romance is finally ready to bloom!

As a coup de grace, Mike foreshadows his intentions to become Howard's son-in-law by shaking hands and saying "Thanks, Dad," before taking Billie to the party. (For her part, it's not unrealistic to predict that by the end of the week Billie will be writing "Mrs. Mike Benson" all over the inside cover of her loose-leaf binder!)

GG: Honesty gets him nowhere, so he follows Howard's old-fashioned advice, gets tough and commanding with Billie ("Hold it!"), and the girl naturally responds. Face it, progressives of both genders… it's never about the battle of the sexes; it's always about the taming of the shrew. Some quaint and comfortable sexist theories never change, even in the usually clear-thinking 21st Century.

DOES BILLIE WIN OR LOSE THE ARGUMENT?

GG: In all fairness, it's something of a draw. Mike gets forceful with Billie, it's true, but it's mainly to tell her that she's a superior human being… a slightly progressive variation of Howard's tried-and-true Be Firm approach. Once put in her place, and despite a point-blank acknowledgment of her superiority, Billie instinctively looks up to her boyfriend/daddy substitute with vulnerable, trusting eyes. Ah, such bliss! "You'll find that being a girl is an easy adjustment to make," her relatively hip Mom recently advised. Easy indeed, especially if you enjoy taking a back seat in life.

CB: Athletes often say a game resulting in a tie score is like 'kissing your sister'. I agree that the showdown between Billie and Mike is far more than simply a 'draw'. When both parties feel understood and each is beyond happy the outcome, the more appropriate way to characterize the result is: 'win-win'. Although I concede Billie feels like it was more her victory than his.

After all, Billie starts out as a tomboy, slow dancing with shaggy dog, feeling like a "lonely little in-between." At the conclusion of her argument with Mike, look at her now: cool teenager dancing with her awesome hot boyfriend at the party.

Billie sings her feelings as the movie ends: "Just to be a girl is my biggest victory!" Amen, my sister!

GG: Here's the big disagree: "Just to be a girl" in mid-'60s America meant abandoning your dreams and career interests (unnatural for females anyway, most felt) in order to find a substitute daddy who will take care of you and the little ones you will soon produce. The perfectly sane and fair idea of a woman pursuing lofty goals *and* having a significant other in her life, along with an eventual family, is never even considered. It took many brave women and men to change this regressive mindset, and we now live in an era where young girls have the same unlimited career choices as their male counterparts.

And to that and the spirit of true freedom, I say, Amen, all of us!

CB: And I say follow your heart! Other considerations may be important, but they will always be secondary. What Billie has found is true love and self-acceptance. It doesn't get much better than that, as far as I can see.

Her Greatest Victory?

At that moment Agnes walks in, prompting Billie to show off gentleman caller Mike Benson. "Look, Mom. I got a real live date," she says with glistening eyes, recalling their recent conversation.

"Wonderful," offers Agnes, smiling warmly.

Meanwhile, Mike turns to Howard with a grateful grin. "Thanks, Dad."

"It's all right, son," Howard answers proudly, quite pleased that even a modified version of his advice seems to have put the smile back on his daughter's face.

Later that night at the Carol victory dinner, dressed-up Billie shares a slow dance with her Dad. And the little heartfelt chat they have seems to put everything in perspective.

"I want to tell you that up until tonight I've been very wrong about something," he gently admits.

"What?"

"You and me."

"What do you mean?"

"You know back at the house when you said to Mike 'You're just like every other man'? You meant me, didn't you?"

"No, I didn't."

"Yes you did. I understand. I'm gonna be a much better friend in the future."

"Daddy? May I tell you a secret?"

"Yeah, sure."

"Being a girl is so much fun, I've decided to give up track…"

"Is that what you want?"

"Yeah."

"Then that's what you should do."

"May I always tell you my secrets?"

"Billie, I hope you will but I know you won't."

"Why not?"

"Because tonight I'm the man you love. One of these days I'll just be your father."

"I don't understand."

"You will."

After a while, dancing partners are changed. Billie couples up with Mike, while mayor-elect Howard and his wife Agnes ease into a comforting once-around.

"Say, did you know that Billie is giving up track?" Howard informs her.

"No, but that's funny, 'cause so is Mike."

"Mike? Poor male of the species…"

"Darling! You sound so sad."

"Well, I am."

"Why?"

"Well, Jeannie's married. She'll be leaving home soon. Billie's no longer a little girl. She'll only be with us a few more years… and then I'm going to become a grandfather."

"Well, look at it this way," a bemused Agnes says pragmatically. "You're not losing a daughter. You're gaining a law partner. You're not losing a track star. You're gaining a daughter. You're not only going to be a grandfather, but also mayor of the town. You're also going to become a father again. *I'm gonna have a baby!*"

Howard's mouth drops at least three feet. "A baby?!"

"Yeah."

"You mean this whole mess is gonna start all over again?"

"That's right."

The Mayor-Elect of Harding is amazed, overwhelmed, and overjoyed. "I'll never survive it," he laughs, shaking his weary head.

"Of course you will," Agnes responds philosophically. "Besides, maybe this time it'll be a boy."

They embrace. And as a happy future is envisioned for the Carols and their newest family member, Beat Maiden Billie Carol, pretty in pink and on her first official grown-up date, celebrates this new side of her persona.

I am a girl that's a girl
And I'm proud as I can be
Just to be glad I'm a girl
It's my greatest victory

I am a girl that's a girl
That's what I intend to be!

The Story

WHAT ARE WE TO MAKE OF BILLIE GIVING UP TRACK?

CB: Let's remember the words of Scripture, via this song by Pete Seeger: *"To everything (turn, turn, turn), There is a season (turn, turn, turn) And a time for every purpose under heaven."*

Billie as tomboy was Billie in the waning moments of a very happy childhood. But then her world turned – and she turned away from childhood games. To say that Billie 'gave up' track is overstating what really happened. Do youngsters 'give up' tricycles? No, they just outgrow them – physically and developmentally, a bicycle becomes the toy of choice. So it is with our heroine – she simply has outgrown her desire to compete on an all-male track team.

Billie sings about the "funny little butterflies" that are the harbinger of her inner transformation. The butterfly serves as a fitting metaphor for the journey our heroine takes from caterpillar (tomboy) to butterfly (young woman). Staying on the track team for grown-up Billie would be like the butterfly ignoring its wings and returning to a caterpillar crawl.

Like her sister Jeannie, Billie is a headstrong young woman who will follow her own bliss! When she tells her Dad she wants to quit the team, Howard asks her exactly the right question: "Is this what *you* really want?" He respects her decision once he knows that it is truly her choice, not a compromise she's being coerced into by an external force. The greatest gifts he can give his beloved daughter in this new phase of her development are acceptance, trust and autonomy. She made a valid choice, and as a wise parent he stands behind her.

GG: As many have pointed out, *Billie*'s third act betrays every forward-thinking notion the movie has been preaching for an hour-and-a-half. A young woman blessed with such exceptional athletic talent that it lands her on the cover of *Life* magazine is giving up a potentially groundbreaking future in sports because… well… she's "grown out of her tomboy phase" and would rather date, and presumably marry and serve, the first boy who takes a romantic interest in her? Say *what?!* It never occurs to anyone that Billie can simply go on in the direction she's headed, make athletic and social history, improve American society in general by her example, get rich, whatever... and also marry Mike, a decent-enough guy who seems to love her no matter what she chooses to do.

Yes, teenagers should be allowed to experiment with their interests and dreams... One week our daughter wants to be a ballerina, the next she's thinking about deep-sea diving as a profession. Fine; figure yourself out... there's a big, bright wonderful world to explore, and there are no truly wrong choices. And that includes your possible future as a homemaker. But for gosh sakes, don't limit yourself before you've even gotten started, don't throw away a miraculous, supremely satisfying natural gift without considering the alternatives.

Sorry, Howard, but telling your daughter "Is that what you want? Then that's what you should do," may be democratic-sounding, but it simply isn't enough. She's a teenager. You're an adult. Mature guidance is required here, that's what Billie is aching for. The fact that Howard Carol is culturally incapable of providing Billie with intelligent options speaks volumes about the tragic limitations of conservative social thinking. In today's more enlightened world, exceptional athlete Billie Carol would be encouraged to become a celebrated and inspirational record-breaker, with unlimited personal and professional potential. In 1965 America, she'll become a housewife, and leave 'changing the world' to someone else.

From this perspective, and in the final analysis, Billie cannot help but register as more sell-out than role model, despite all her initial crusading. But the fault lies not with this beautiful, intelligent, inquisitive human being, but with an unconsciously repressive super-society that, guided by well-intentioned ignorance, manages to crush her spirited individuality. For the moment.

Patty Duke as "Billie"

WHAT ARE WE TO MAKE OF MIKE GIVING UP TRACK?

GG: The guy's a sweetheart, and gets points for giving up track because the person he loves is giving up track, and he doesn't want to remind Billie of her sacrifice. Of course, Mike wasn't very good as a runner, whereas the super-charged Ms. Carol is so fantastic she's already on the cover of *Life*. So what appears to be a mutual sacrifice is actually a tad one-sided upon closer examination. But hey, the tomboy's grown out of her awkward stage, discovered the joys of romance, she'll probably make a good wife and mother, so all is right with the world. The '65 world, anyway.

CB: Mike quitting the track team is actually a sacrifice on his part, but it's one he's more than willing to make in the true spirit of compromise. For Mike, the all male track and field team certainly was an acceptable outlet for physical activity. However, looking at the big picture, Mike decided that discretion would be the better part of valor – and besides, he could use The Beat to rev up for a swim meet or a run on the gridiron!

•••

And so the Great Discourse is over, such as it was. Thanks for putting up with us. All gimmickry aside, I hope these comments and counter-comments inspired some worthwhile thinking, and I apologize if Casey and I got a little carried away at times.

Now I have a confession to make.

Instead of merely re-visiting this argument and taking the sides we took back in '77, Casey suggested that we embrace an exercise every writer is taught in college: reverse your point-of-view, and fight just as vigorously for the opposing argument. We upped the ante by taking things to the next level, mixing and matching what we really believed with equally-plausible counter-theories. For the record, I was the one who defended Billie's right to put on her pink dress in that 1977 discussion, progressive politics be damned, while

Casey was horrified by the social sell-out. Now, many decades later, the two of us recognized that the smartest way to 'get at the truth' was to literally take all sides, and hopefully some worthwhile observations might emerge from that. Hopefully, some did.

Next: More about the movie's impact when it was first released, and a plethora of additional contemporary opinions from some pretty amazing thinkers…

3 Cols. x 105 Lines—315 Lines (23 Inches) Mat 303

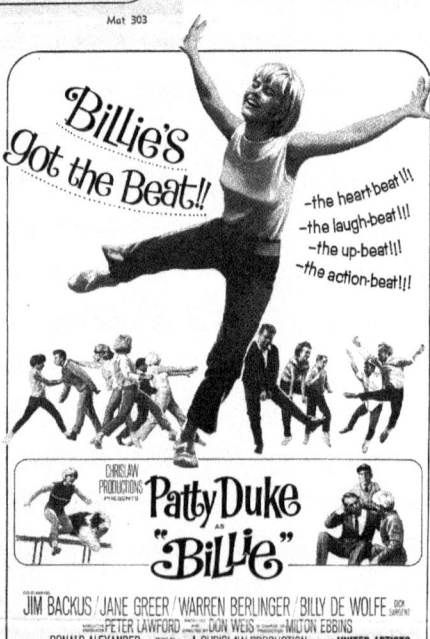

Selling and Seeing "Billie"

Pressbook Newspaper Ads

PRESSBOOKS, AKA EXHIBITOR'S MANUALS, ARE PROVIDED BY THE FILM STUDIO to help local theaters get the most out of their product. Among the various visual elements on display are a plethora of newspaper ads, in all sizes and shapes, that reflect the movie's advertising campaign. Here are two such ads for *Billie*, the second pretty much a duplication of the one-sheet poster used.

Illustrated Poster Key Art

Mitchell Hooks

Frank Frazetta (unused)

PATTY DUKE AS "BILLIE"

Pressbook Ballyhoo

Pressbooks traditionally offered exhibitors a wide array of publicity suggestions, most of them pretty outlandish. Opposite page: various Patty Duke record releases tied in with *Billie*, including albums and singles.

Typical Teenage Room

"Billie," as played by Patty Duke, being a typical teen-ager, her bedroom is a typical teen-ager's and therein lies a good possibility for a window or lobby "bedroom" in the furnishing of which a number of co-operating merchants can participate.

In order for it to be typical "Billie," co-operation calls for more than furniture. There should be phonographs, hi-fi's, typewriters, skis, basket balls, tennis racquets, fan magazines, riding habits; dog leashes, combs, feeding pans, fishing equipment, and anything else you can think of which would be of interest to a pre-dating teen-ager of about 16. Cards carry names of co-operating merchants.

Get The Whole Town Whooping It Up For 'Billie' With Ballyhoo Built Around Athletics, Dances

INVITATION TO COACH: An invitation from Athletic Coach Jones of Harding High School — the coach and school of "Billie" — to the coach of a local high school to come down and see how things are done in his school, particularly on the girls, can be the basis for a school athletic rally at your theatre.

The latter can accept in several ways. He can send a drill team from his school, made up of girls of course, or he can send a team to do some intricate ball passing either on your stage, in your lobby or in an adjacent athletic field during an intermission in some sort of athletic activity.

Or, preferably on opening night, he can send down his band and drum majorettes (possibly for a street parade, "We're on our way to show up BILLIE!") and cheer leaders for a lobby, marquee or stage show.

DECATHLON CONTEST: A "Billie Decathlon" to discover once and for all if girls are as good as boys at athletics, particularly field events, should provide a lot of excitement, fun and publicity.

Meet, of course, is based right on the plot of "Billie," the tomboy type played by Patty Duke, and this can "inspire" the test. It can be run as either a city-wide meet, with every school, club, girl and boy scout troop or what-have-you providing contestants of both sexes, or it can be held in conjunction with a neighborhood or school fieldday, picnic or outing. Co-operation may be sought from sporting goods distributors, physical fitness groups.

'BILLIE' AS MASCOT: Get a girl team in town—(baseball, handball, basketball)—to "adopt" "Billie" as its mascot! A photo of the team standing around a photoblowup of Patty Duke as "Billie" should make the sports page of the local newspaper or get some time on a local TV news-sports broadcast.

LOCAL 'BILLIES'— Your community can probably supply a number of girls of the "Billie" type—pre-dating teenagers somewhat on the tomboyish side and excellent at athletics—and it may be an idea to round up a flock of 'em for a TV oneshot in which the local "Billies" can be interviewed against giant blowup background of posters from the picture. Of course, if any of them happens to be named "Billie," you've got an extra dividend on the promotion value of the gimmick.

'BILLIE' DANCE PARTY: This picture literally screams for a local record hop. Announce a Saturday afternoon party called the "Billy Hop" and decorate the studio (or gym) with album covers, stills from the picture, posters and anything else that smacks of teen agers, athletics, dances, etc. Award prizes for dancers in singles, pairs or groups.

Selling and Seeing "Billie"

Albums and Singles

EXPLOITATION MATERIAL

PATTY DUKE VOCAL, SOUND TRACK ALBUM KEY BIG MUSIC CAMPAIGN!

The music from "Billie"—from the pen of famed Dominic Frontiere—is nothing short of terrific, and as sung by Patty Duke it's colossal!

Which is by way of warming you up to the possibilities afforded by the recordings from United Artists Records which will be available from this picture!

They are a Sound Track Album, a single "Funny Little Butterflies" by Patty Duke, and another single of the title song "Billie."

All of this warrants as intensive a music co-op campaign as you've ever waged! It should mean windows, disc-jock co-operation, juke box stacking, gifts to record editors, PA plugging wherever you can get it, and anything and everything else you've ever done to exploit a picture via its music!

Remember: Patty Duke is one of TV's most popular stars! Her following runs into the millions and a large segment of it lives right in your town!

Reception

Given its meager goals and overall inoffensiveness, *Billie* earned reasonably kind critical notices. No one was fooled into thinking this little quickie was anything other than what it purported to be, a cute and harmless way to cash in on Patty Duke's popularity with the teen set. The social elements that would one day make *Billie* such an oddball touchstone for debate were barely grasped by '65 reviewers, unsurprisingly. As with the various incarnations of *Time Out for Ginger* proper, critics missed all the provocative implications, instead focusing on light-hearted, familiar comical elements and *Billie*'s abundance of family warmth. Richard F. Shepard's review for *The New York Times* (September 16, 1965) is fairly typical:

•••

"BILLIE" BEGINS RUN

"BILLIE", a rosy-cheeked teenage comedy starring Patty Duke, opened yesterday at neighborhood theaters, where it is a perfectly harmless placebo.

Paced by an experienced cast and direction, the movie is along the lines of what is kindly called family situation comedy on television. Old Dad, played by Jim Backus, speaks one way about how daughters should behave as young ladies, but is benign when it comes to his younger offspring becoming a track star on a high school team composed of boys. There are moments of amusement, but enough is too much.

In 1952 the original version of *Billie* made its debut on Broadway as *Time Out For Ginger*, by Ronald Alexander, a deft writer who has also done this screen play.

It drew felicitous reviews as stage fare, but maybe they should have broken the mold then and there. After years of similar situations, the film offers nothing new. Miss Duke, Mr. Backus and Warren Berlinger, as the boyfriend, are beguiling, there is one good lively bit of choreography in a locker room, and that's about it. Still and all, what with its rock 'n' roll rhythm and its dependence on a mental 'beat' that prods the girl runner to winning form, it will probably appeal to mid-teenagers who are looking for diversion from homework.

•••

Not exactly a ringing endorsement, but no worse and probably a little better than notices for similar teenage confections of the day. Having dazzled the world with *The Miracle Worker*, Patty Duke was favored by film critics, and even *The Patty Duke Show* was tolerated, as it raised the bar for teen actresses because of the relatively challenging double-role. It was a lot harder to defend something like *Billie*, but the Ronald Alexander pedigree and *Time Out for Ginger*'s positive reputation helped.

Box Office and Beyond

Part of United Artists' Premiere Showcase rollout, *Billie* earned $1,500,000 during its initial North American theatrical release. That was somewhat less than what Chrislaw was hoping for, but when coupled with record-related profits and a groundbreaking TV sale (to NBC, rather than Duke's home network ABC), and factoring in the miniscule budget, *Billie* scored well enough to be classified as a modest hit.

The picture eventually ran on NBC's *Tuesday Night at the Movies* skein (February 10, 1970), and was repeated later in the season. New York critic Judith Crist, writing a regular column for *TV Guide* at the time where she overviewed each week's network movie offerings, pooh-poohed the sitcom flavors of *Billie*, literally asking why an actress of Duke's stature would waste her considerable talents on such innocuous material.

Again, this was a little too early for mainstreamers to look beyond *Billie*'s superficial pleasures... a new generation of film fans and analyzers, more sophisticated, certainly more cynical, and prone to revealing hidden truths about the often hypocritical underbelly of Greatest Generation achievement, would find in the movie a plethora of coded themes and meanings.

Goofed on for its *Gidget*-like innocence, but eventually embraced by the gay counter-culture very much the way Doris Day's tomboy turn in *Calamity Jane* was (Day's 1953 hit song "Secret Love," meant as a romantic ode to suitor Bill Hickok, was instantly adopted as a powerful gay anthem), *Billie* suddenly found the same meaning read into "Lonely Little In-Between." And with good reason. The inherent angst of the song is universal, and especially resonant with alienated youth. Duke's heartfelt delivery makes this painfully personal call for help convincing, whatever meaning one ascribes to it.

Beyond the always-intriguing social angle, *Billie* has recently picked up some small measure of respect as one of a small group of 'full-out teen musicals', a genre that combines the high-spirited physicality of mid-'60s rock pop/go-go music with the equally 'up' fundamentals of Broadway showstoppers. The results can be obtuse and ultra-campy, but fearless production numbers in movies like *Billie, Summer Holiday,* and *The Cool Ones* are refreshingly artful when viewed today. *Billie*'s semi-inherited (from United Artists) *West Side Story* pedigree (which meant some talented dancers) added to the film's retro-luster as a Hollywood pop musical of merit, while the presence and participation of *Shindig/Hullabaloo* talent and Broadway's much-celebrated Donna McKechnie provided additional positive layers.

As the cliché goes, no one will ever mistake *Billie* for an exceptional piece of cinema, or even a great musical film. But its winning combination of raw talent on energetic display, in both the musical and athletic sequences (credit Duke's stunt double for some amazing feats, in long shot), and the aforementioned 'meanings' viewers are fond of reading into it, keeps this odd little family movie retro-relevant.

The Controversy

YEARS PASSED AFTER CASEY AND I HAD OUR LEGENDARY DISCUSSION ABOUT Billie Carol's profound lifestyle decision, and neither one of us thought much about it. Then, by chance circa late '80s, I happened to notice some interesting comments about the film in a British media magazine discussing changing social attitudes as reflected in popular culture... the first sighting of a *Billie*-related think piece. Was it possible that other minds found intellectual interest in this seemingly featherweight family confection? It appeared *Billie* was suddenly worthy of debate as either a pre-feminist rant that chickens out in its final lap, or an unconsciously closeted exploration of homosexual angst.

Not surprisingly, the Internet age completely opened up these ideological floodgates, enabling civilians of all stripes, along with the pros, to weigh in with opinions. IMDb viewer responses, official studio boards, DVD reviews, Patty Duke fan sites, and many other public venues were suddenly alive with colorful conclusions about Billie Carol's social integrity and sexual identity.

The fact that Duke followed this Disney-like romp with her infamous turn as vindictive, self-obsessed diva Neely O'Hara in *Valley of the Dolls* just added to *Billie*'s growing reputation as a cultural oddity worth revisiting.

What follows now is a smorgasbord of opinion, conjecture and speculation. In some cases, the writers are clearly professionals offering focused, detailed analyses in their essays to support fresh insights. Other responses are more like spontaneous sound bites, though no less potent and passionate. We'll begin with some very astute essays, the first of these even inspiring one of the film's principal cast members to respond.

DVD TALK: BILLIE by Bill Gibron, May 31, 2004

Championing equality is a relatively recent development in the social structure, an impractical idiom for the white male-dominated domain that honestly should have been embraced eons ago. The concept that we would purposefully treat people differently because of their sex, race or belief system is about as shallow and illogical as ideologies get. Why not pick something even more superficial, like hair color or wine preference? One's heritage or biological limits should never dismiss them from opportunity, but for decades, these obvious attributes have been paraded out as reasons why certain sectors of the communal order are allowed the privilege of Constitutional consideration. This trickle down theory of due process has provided our country with some of its most vicious internal fighting, as well as some of our more enigmatic leaders. Without the wisdom and sacrifice of these brave defenders of human dignity, we'd still be living in a land of segregation, subjugation and 'separate by equal'.

No one will be hurrying to place Billie Carol up on the Mt. Rushmore of race/gender equity anytime soon. This tomboy with a taste for the Mersey beat believes that gals have every right to participate on the boys' track team (so far, so good). She challenges her politician father to explain away this grave inequity, especially considering how good she is at the sport. He can't

(still batting 1000). She even finds like-minded individuals who champion her desire to compete on an equal footing (like her coach and her mother. Bravo, Billie). But before we declare this high school hotfoot the Susan B. Anthony of athletics, it's important to understand just where this activist agenda comes from. Is Billie a pioneer of scholastic civil disobedience? No. Is she on a quest to pave the way for true unprejudiced access to sports for all little ladies? Nope. Is it merely a matter of standing up for what's right, in spite of what everyone else thinks? Yes, but sadly that is beside the point.

All Billie really wants is fatherly affection and a bo-hunky boyfriend. And she wants to sing about it as well. It's this miscalculation of mixed musical messages that makes balderdash out of Billie's beliefs. And the movie named after her so terribly uneven.

Saccharine, syrupy and dipped in a slick show business coating of convenient convolutions, *Billie* is the 1965, Disney-fied version of an 'issue' film, the kind of made for TV cinema that Lifetime and Oxygen currently specialize in. Taken from the play *Time Out for Ginger* (which begs the question, who is Ginger and why was the character's name changed to Billie) it's a movie that attempts to address the, at the time, rising interest in feminism and equal rights by handing out sheet music and letting the characters break out in song... well, a couple of songs. *Billie* is posited as a musical, but it's more like a muddle with pop tones. We get a melody in the intro, a solo ballad for young star Patty Duke (sitting pretty on a hit TV show and her Oscar for *The Miracle Worker*) reconfigured in two different versions and a *Can't Stop the Music* style all male locker room romp (talk about being ahead of its time). But this is not a case of music moving the storyline. Indeed, the melodies seem like an afterthought, a way of changing what was probably a much fiercer statement on civil rights onstage into a borderline boring bit of beach blanket jingoism aimed squarely at the too hip for this trip youth market. In combination with the scattershot agenda, exceptional acting and overall vibrant energy, *Billie* becomes a puzzle. It works in spite of itself, but also fails because of its very strengths.

As for its cast, *Billie* offers old-fashioned Hollywood spunk and specialty at its very best. Proving he was properly paired with power players like James Dean and Natalie Wood in *Rebel Without a Cause*, Jim Backus manages the near impossible feat of balancing an extremely sexist viewpoint about the male/female dynamic with a good natured sense of compromise. He's nowhere near the tacky tastiness of *Gilligan's Island*'s Thurston Howell III, but he manages to make us care about his character, even as he spouts his barefoot and pregnant viewpoint. As his long-suffering wife, Jane Greer has very little dialogue, forced to express all her inner feelings through eye movement and body language. Partly as a result of a battle with palsy at age 15 – an illness that left part of her face paralyzed – Greer's command of her facial gesturing is magical and makes Mr. Carol a compassionate, if passive, persona. Equally effective is Warren Berlinger, who many will probably remember from hundreds of TV appearances, as the young boy with a broken heart over his mixed emotions for Billie. On the one hand, he finds her attractive and caring. On the other, he is still under the influence of the paternalistic society he was raised in, believing that he could only go with a gal if she were a subservient shrinking violet. Along with familiar faces like Ted Bessell (*That Girl*), Richard Deacon (*The Dick Van Dyke Show*) and Billy De Wolfe (a favorite fey villain in Uncle Walt's live action vault), the amount of talent here is impressive and completely understandable for a mid-'60s Hollywood movie.

But this is really Patty Duke's showcase, and it's amazing how exceptional she is in her underwritten role. She almost single-handedly saves this middling movie. *Billie* still manages to fall apart and barely bumble across the finish line, but if there were a reason to sit through this cinematic time trial, it would be the effervescent child star. Impressive from a very young age, her turn in *The Miracle Worker* is still one of the best performances by a teenage actress onscreen. But few remember how ebullient and complicated her characters of Patty/Cathy, identical twin cousins, were on *The Patty Duke Show* (probably because they can't get past the now classic camp lyrics to the theme song "Patty likes to rock and roll/a hot dog makes her lose control", Oh my). Only a year and a half before she'd tear up the soundstages as Neely O'Hara in Jacqueline Susann's potboiler *Valley of the Dolls*, (and begin an impressive self-destructive phase as a little girl lost in a trashy tabloid Tinsel Town) *Billie* is best considered a middle motion picture, a placeholder for Duke in the Hollywood pecking order until she grew out of her awkward phase and grasped young adulthood by the script choice. Today, Duke is probably best known as either the mother of 'fat hobbit' Sean 'Samwise' Astin or as a manic-depressive victim of abuse, a molested mess who used to sleep in her own urine and feces, if you believe her tantalizing autobiography *Call*

Me Anna. But she was (and according to the wealth of weepy TV movies she's made, still is) a glorious, gifted performer and *Billie* is a bubbly showcase for this unique talent.

It's just too bad that the movie couldn't have been more focused. When it's serious about the social issue of equality and women's rights, it's fresh and effective. There are debates between the mayoral candidates about freedom and gender equity – along with occasional battles on the home front – that present both sides of the age old argument with dignity and decision. Problem is, once we are handed the solemn, the silly can't be far behind and *Billie* blows its political points with hokey jokes about locker rooms and liberation. *Time Out for Ginger* may have handled this material in a more mature manner, but *Billie* can only address it within a certain set of power point parameters. Get too aggressive in the agenda and it's time for some slapstick. The friction in the family unit is also explored with heart and honesty. Jim Backus' Howard Carol has a bad habit of calling his daughter 'son', an obvious insight into his desire to have a heritage providing all the athletic pride to the family, not his teenybopper daughter. Billie's whole demeanor suggests a child trying to fit into her father's image of who she is, and that struggle, when explored, is very well done. Duke has a line where, after asking her aghast father if he loves her, she breaks out of the perky and shows the inner pain she is feeling. It's a moment so moving, so steeped in truth that we start to see what this movie is really supposed to be about. But then *Billie* has to go and cloud the concepts, undermining everything with vicious over plotting (the whole grown sister/marriage/scandal issue), the introduction of broad, buffoonish ancillary characters and lame, lumbering show tunes.

Indeed, the rock 'n' roll angle, used to sell this movie both at the time of it's release and on the DVD version, is woefully underdeveloped. Billie says she has 'The Beat', a typical 60s drum riff that makes her run faster than everyone else. Huh? How does that work, exactly? If it's merely a matter of listening to a ready steady rhythm in your head, why doesn't it work for everyone? Is this just a sheltered way of saying that Billie is really physically better than

the boys on the team, and the PMA (positive *musical* attitude) she uses to excuse her excellence is a form of veiled self-denial? Who knows? All we really get are a couple of bogus British invasion instrumental numbers and a dance hall tutorial where Billie tries to impart her foot stomping on the rest of the gang. These goofy, gangly time wasters are obvious inserts, attempts by

Hollywood to jazz up the adolescent angst inherent in a high school portion of the plot. The music is the most obvious awkward fit into the format of this movie. After a poignant moment between father and daughter, Billie will take to the auditorium stage and bounce around like she's auditioning for Bob Fosse's next show. The dance numbers can be excused, since the role of rock in mid-'60s lifestyle had everyone onscreen doing the frug. But vocalizing is another issue all together. Sadly, Duke is no singer, and her horrible warbling of the main languid lament "Funny Little In-between/ Butterflies" makes other child star singers seem like Sinatra. Still, her acting really sells the songs and it's this divergent dichotomy that keeps *Billie* from going completely belly-up. It also provides the properties that keep it awash in waves of wasted opportunities.

Billie wants to be something both challenging and cheery, a movie that makes its pointed political positions with genuineness and gentility. But it also wants to play in the arena of the adolescent, selling its shaggy dog antisexism with far too much formulaic foolishness. The message of this messy motion picture is plain and simple: people should be allowed to explore their own options in life, left to learn what fits them, and their gender, best. But it's buried in a bunch of situation comedy cornball conventions that all but destroy the dogma. If it weren't for the fine acting and the fleeting glimpses of genuine compassion, *Billie* would be a bust, a tired trinket in the forgotten canon of Patty Duke's post-child stardom. If it had mined the real issue of gender equality and equal rights, it would have been a heralded example of ahead of its time testifying. But thanks to the inclusion of soundtrack fattening facets and a substantial chunk of stage play clunkiness, *Billie* can't get its particular point across. Instead, this movie has about as many flawed facets as its star would soon battle in real life. *Billie* is not a complete waste of time. But with this cast, there must have been a better story to tell than this one.

Billie would be a very easy film to dismiss. It's sappy when it should be sharp, winsome when it needs to be wise. It believes that all young girls, if given a chance to compete on a equal footing with the boys, will realize the error of their overreaching ways and be content to represent their sex as prom dates and cheerleaders, not captains of the athletic teams. It's steeped in the paternalistic mythos that women don't know what they want and can't understand how hard it is to be a male in a man's world. And it believes, much like *Parenthood* or *She's Having a Baby*, that biology and the birthing of a brat makes everything sunny and bright. With this antiquated agenda pushing its buttons, *Billie* should insult more people than it empowers. But somehow, over all the hot button issues and Elvis-level production numbers, this political piffle is enjoyable and genuine. And it's thanks, in no small part, to the pitch perfect acting of the ensemble here. Sure, Duke holds the majority of the movie with her blond pageboy moxie, but it's the winning support she gets from the rest of the cast, mixed with moments of sentiment and spirit that recommend this otherwise routine film. *Billie* may not have helped advance the Title 9 mentality sweeping through competitive athletics, but it understood one simple thing. People should be treated as equals, even if they aren't alike on the inside or the out. There's nothing wrong with that message. Nothing at all.

On May 17, 2013, Warren Berlinger (Mike Benson) responded:

> Mr. Gibron! Thank you for the opportunity (albeit late) to admire, respect and enjoy your review of *Billie*. (It's a) homage to critics of substance and quality.
>
> Being a survivor of this cast, it is important to recognize the import of the subject matter and the passion of that period. (It's akin to) the experience, a few years earlier on Broadway, of *Blue Denim*, dealing with abortion (never mentioned before on B'way) and the scars, slings and you know what our cast suffered through.
>
> The peeling of the onion is still in process.
>
> My thanks and very good wishes, Warren Berlinger.

Patty Duke as "Billie"

THE CONTROVERSY

DREAMS ARE WHAT LE CINEMA IS FOR: BILLIE (1965)
by Ken Anderson, December 19, 2013

A favorite little-known Patty Duke film (perhaps deservedly so) sandwiched innocuously between her Oscar-winning turn in *The Miracle Worker* (1962) and the near career-killing ignominity of *Valley of the Dolls* (1967) – which has become, most assuredly, THE film she'll be most remembered for – is *Billie*: a sprightly, featherweight, teen musical about a tomboyish track and field dynamo suffering with gender-identity issues.

I won't kid you, the above description, as brief as it is, makes *Billie* sound considerably more substantial than it is. Point in fact: clocking in at a brisk 87 minutes, *Billie* is so lightweight it's barely there... which, in my book, makes it the perfect vehicle for when you want to see a movie, but aren't looking for much in the way of substance. Kind of like the cinematic equivalent of a schnecken. It's not a motion picture so much as a big screen TV sitcom padded out to feature length with a few lively musical numbers and what easily has to be fifteen minutes' worth of reaction shot cutaways to the family sheepdog.

As is the case with so many 60s sitcoms, the plot of *Billie* hinges on a single, silly gimmick. In this instance, in lieu of talking horses, identical twin cousins, or mothers reincarnated as automobiles; we have an average teenager who, thanks to a bit of a mind flip called 'The Beat' – the ability to hear a rhythm in her head and transfer that percussive beat into athletic prowess – is able to outrun, out jump, and outperform every male member of her highschool track team.

If you're scratching your head wondering how, unless the story is set in *Downtown Abbey*, a feature film's worth of comic/dramatic conflict can be wrung from a non-issue like a female athlete in 1965; it helps to know that *Billie* is adapted from a wheezy 1952 stage play by Ronald Alexander titled *Time Out for Ginger*, and, save for the substituting of track & field for the play's inter-gender football premise, makes it to the screen with its outmoded sexual politics intact. (Although, when compared to the princess-fixated,

Pepto-Bismol pink vision of femininity marketed to young girls today, *Billie*'s fairly toothless challenge to the male/female status quo of 1965 is practically a feminist manifesto.) In addition, research for this post revealed to me that until federal sex discrimination laws were passed in 1972, athletic programs for girls were a very low priority in many high schools. So perhaps some aspects of *Billie*'s plot aren't as far-fetched as I once thought.

Mayoral candidate Howard Carol (Backus) resides in a house full of women, yet runs his campaign on a 'return to gentility', anti-women's rights platform. Agnes (Greer), his long-suffering wife, is one of those wisely sardonic housewives typical of 60s sitcoms: she's genuinely smarter than her husband, but regularly defers to his oafishness out of love and an understanding of the fragility of the male ego. Eldest daughter, Jeannie (Susan Seaforth), is the ultra-femme apple of Howard's eye and the veritable poster girl for non-threatening, 60s womanhood. Not only does she look like a younger model of her mother, but at age 20 she wants nothing more from life than to quit college, marry, and get down to the business of making babies. Goals her character has already achieved by the time she's first introduced.

This leaves fifteen-year-old Billie (Duke), a self-professed "lonely little in-between" wrestling with puberty and grappling with anxiety over her gender-identification. And small wonder. She has a father who clearly favors her pretty and feminine older sister, and in this painful exchange, accidentally lets slip how he really feels about his youngest offspring:

Father: "From now on, try to remember that you're a girl!"
Billie: "I wish I was a boy…"
Father: "So do I, but you're not!"
Ouch! I understand the title for the sequel is: *Time Out for Therapy*.

When Billie is later recruited by the high school track coach ("*…to shame the boys into trying harder*"), her newfound notoriety as the team's most valuable player not only threatens to alienate potential suitor, Mike Benson (the doughy Warren Berlinger), but derail her reluctantly supportive father's run for mayor. What's a girl/boy to do?

Patty Duke as "Billie"

What I Love About this Film

Unless, like me, you're a nostalgia-prone boomer who grew up on white-bread, middle-class, suburban family comedies of the 60s, and nursed a prepubescent crush on cute-as-a-button Patty Duke; *Billie* is a movie so dated and obviously aimed at kids, you're apt to find it more trying than entertaining. (Although, I ask you, who can resist that infectious soundtrack?)

Given what must have been a pretty tight shooting schedule, *Billie* is pretty straightforward stuff as far as filmmaking goes. There's no art to the cinematography beyond making sure everyone remains within the frame and everything is in focus. The editing is of the ping-pong variety: alternating medium shots of whomever is talking in a particular scene. There's not even much to say about the performances, as everyone does a professional, workmanlike job with their sketchily written parts. So what, beyond the overall competence of the endeavor, do I enjoy about *Billie*?

The fact that each time I revisit it, its surface simplicity begins to look more complex.

Like a great many family-oriented films that haven't aged particularly well, *Billie* has evolved over the years into one of those cult-worthy, meta-movies that, when viewed through the prism of contemporary mores, can't help but operate on several different levels simultaneously. Most of them inadvertent. All of them more interesting than the film as originally conceived.

There's *Billie* the high-school musical and puberty allegory about a confused tomboy teetering on the brink of womanhood; *Billie* the insincere social-conflict farce that pays lip service to women's equality, yet in its heart really believes that men and women are just happier occupying traditional gender roles; *Billie* the 'very special episode' of the *ABC Afterschool Special* about a transgender teen struggling with being a boy trapped in a girl's body (the most persuasive layer, if you ask me); and, finally, *Billie* the 'be yourself' *Glee* episode about the growing pains of a latent lesbian high-school track star (Duke's resemblance to Ellen Degeneres adding yet *another* layer).

An uncomfortable layer, but one the good-natured actress is more than willing to attest to these days, is the curious fact that, given her real-life battle with bipolarism, she was so often cast in roles that required her to play dueling sides of her own personality.

Performances

Thanks to reruns of *The Patty Duke Show* airing currently on Antenna TV, I've had the opportunity to reacquaint myself with what a charming and natural comedienne Patty Duke can be. Her Patty Lane may not have been as glamorous as the teens Elinor Donahue and Shelley Fabares played on *Father Knows Best* and *The Donna Reed Show*, respectively, but she was far more likable, relatable, and a real dynamo of energy (Patty Lane was quite the scrappy little toughie. Episodes highlighting her character's selfish, bossy side show signs of a budding Neely O'Hara).

The talented Patty Duke is undeniably the glue holding *Billie* together (the film is credited to Chrislaw/Patty Duke Productions, Chrislaw being the Peter Lawford-headed production company responsible for *The Patty Duke Show*), but her trademark vitality feels strangely subdued, and the film doesn't really make the most of her talents. Saddled with a character that spends the majority of the film feeling wounded, confused or bewildered, Duke is left shouldering all of the film's dramatic weight (which she handles capably), a lot of its singing (Duke's real voice gets a healthy assist from Lesley Gore-style overdubbing, but she's no Neely O'Hara), some of its dancing (as with her track scenes, doubles are occasionally used), but very little of its comedy.

Regrettably, that's left to the supporting cast of stock characters populated by familiar TV faces. Each relying on the same schticky, sure-fire comedy takes and delivery we've all seen from them a million times before.

I must admit that the pleasure of having the great Jane Greer appear in *Billie* (she's one of my all-time favorite noir femme fatales. *Out of the Past* and *The Big Steal* are absolute must-sees) is mitigated significantly by seeing her lethal brand of smoldering insouciance reduced to playing sweetly supportive back-up to a blowhard character like Jim Backus. Just the kind of male chauvinist sap one of her earlier film noir personas would have tossed into the trunk of an automobile and sent hurtling off a cliff without batting an eyelash.

The Stuff of Fantasy

Should *Billie*'s retro riffs on gender roles grow tiresome, I can always console myself with its dancing. Choreographed by Elvis/*Beach Party* movie stalwart David Winters (*Shindig, Hullabaloo*) in that curiously self-mocking, frenetic style that looks like a hybrid of 60s go-go and traditional musical comedy jazz (popularized in Broadway shows like *Promises, Promises* and *Applause*), these numbers are lively, silly, and a great deal of fun.

Making her film debut (and serving as the film's co-choreographer) is *A Chorus Line*'s Donna McKechnie showing impeccable form in the red-and-white rugby stripes. She, along with director/mentor Michael Bennett, were dancers on the teen variety show, *Hullabaloo*. Several of the dancers in *Billie* are recognizable from 60s-era films like *West Side Story* and *The Unsinkable Molly Brown*. A triple-bill of *Bye Bye Birdie*, *Billie*, and *The Cool Ones* would serve as a terrific primer on the effect of pop music on movie musical choreography.

Overemphatic, "The Girl is a Girl is a Girl" is a musical number that really stuck with me when I was a kid. I wonder why? Wittily staged in a high-school locker room, the amusing and rousing number features lots of chorus boys dancing with each other while trying to act all macho (clenching their hands into fists while singing out of the sides of their mouths) in skimpy 60s gym shorts.

The Stuff of Dreams

While it's hard to imagine that *Billie* did Patty Duke's reputation as an Oscar-winning actress any good, I think it's fair to say it didn't do it much harm, either. In fact, I was surprised to learn that *Billie* was a hit when it came out. A fact no doubt helped by Duke's popularity on the record charts (her

two debut singles, "Don't Just Stand There" and "Say Something Funny" were each Top 40 hits), and propelled by the cross-promotion provided by Duke singing the film's single, "Funny Little Butterflies", on the variety program, *Shindig*, as well as on an episode of her own TV show.

Patty Duke's managers (about whom much has been written) obviously had a vested interest in milking Duke's teenage appeal for as long as they could, and putting her in a disposable pop confection like this must have appeared, if perhaps a bit short-sighted (Duke was fast approaching adulthood), from a professional standpoint, both expedient and profitable. Personally, I would love to have seen her take on *Inside Daisy Clover* (coincidentally, released the same year as *Billie*), a film not only better suited to her talents, but one that might have eased her into adult roles a little more gracefully than *Valley of the Dolls*. (For the record, what with Natalie Wood being a friend of the author and a much bigger star, it's doubtful that Duke would ever have been in the running for *Inside Daisy Clover*.)

Bonus Material

As much as I enjoy this movie, the enduring popularity of Ronald Alexander's play, *Time Out for Ginger*, truly baffles me. At various times in its revival history, the play attracted the talents of Liza Minnelli and Steve McQueen. Go figure. As far as I'm concerned, it's Patty Duke, the '60s music, the dancing, and the time-acquired abstract levels of camp and multiple interpretation that make *Billie*'s thoroughly run-of-the-mill plot even remotely bearable.

By the way, for the benefit of any *Rosemary's Baby* fans out there, playwright Ronald Alexander is also the author of *Nobody Loves an Albatross*.

On Dec. 20, 2013, Poseidon3 posted:

...I remember thinking the first time I saw this that it would make a hooty double bill with *The Christine Jorgensen Story*.

On Dec. 20, 2013, Ken responded:

It's funny you should mention *The Christine Jorgensen Story*, because I was going to match that screencap of Patty Duke in her pink party dress and pouffy hair, with a pic of that thick-necked actor (John Hansen) who starred in it. Neither really looks like a convincing female.

On Dec. 21, 2013, Bitter69uk posted:

Patty certainly does convince as a butch young baby dyke in your above screen grabs.

On Dec. 21, 2013, Ken responded:

"Butch young baby dyke…" Ha! That about sums it up. I'm surprised this movie hasn't been adopted on the LGBT film festival circuit, it's so perfectly a 60s version of a coming-out story masked as a coming of age tale.

ISN'T LIFE TERIBLE? BLOG: PATTY IS DEAD, YOU'RE BILLIE NOW

Billie, ostensibly a "family film", is an alarming look into the depths of gender dyphoria, also known as Gender Identity Disorder (GID). Today, GID is treatable, with gender reassignment surgery. When *Billie* was released in the fall of 1965, between seasons 2 and 3 of *The Patty Duke Show* (itself an exploration of duality), the MPAA code forbade movies on the subject. However, the filmmakers behind *Billie* employed a clever and unusual technique to get their messages across.

In the literary world, the technique is known as 'symbolism'. Developed in the late 19th century, symbolism is a way of exteriorizing (sic) the interiorized (sic) lives of characters by selectively imbuing ordinary household items with hidden, profound levels of meaning.

Patty Duke as "Billie"

When Billie sniffs her track shoes, they are more than track shoes. When Billie pours out her anguish to a stuffed wolf, the audience becomes restless… due not only to Patty Duke's performance, but also to the large photograph of her father, Tyler Fitzgerald, next to her bed. At the end of the song, Billie is left with a stark choice… the smell of the track shoe in her left hand – or – the bottle of perfume in her right? Symbolically, Billie must choose: male, or female? The character literally 'weighs her options'. Indeed, it is from the end of this scene that our modern phrase 'heavy-handed symbolism' is derived.

Billie is 'out of sync' with her world; is it any wonder that, by the end of the clip, her lips are out of sync with the soundtrack?

Duke saw *Billie* as her chance to prove, once and for all, that she could act in color. Eventually, she would move to Idaho.

Two different endings were filmed, and, at great expense, the *Billie* production team reunited all living members of the Pomona audience that attended the first showing of *The Magnificent Ambersons*. The 'Serious Ending' – in which Billie hears that Coach Jones is in the hospital after being hit by an automobile and uses her high-speed running power to reach the operating room in time to donate the muscles in her leg to fashion the coach a new heart – was so disliked that many in the audience suspected that *Billie* had been secretly directed by Orson Welles.

In the released version, Billie quits the track team because 'she likes being a girl' and flees the city with Deckard, whom she suspects is a replicant.

Florence Griffith Joyner, who saw the film at the tender age of 6, has said that she was negatively inspired by Patty Duke's masterful performance and has since credited her Olympic wins to "having The Beat".

For the truly masochistic, the trailer is playing continuously (Look for dancer/choreographer Donna McKechnie in the *Where's Waldo?* shirt).

ISN'T IT DELICIOUS? Feb. 26 2010

Young Patty Duke plays a "lonely little in-between" in the deliciously butch 1960s musical *Billie*.

Let's hope that the 1965 *Billie* is Hollywood's first and final women's lib track-and-field teen musical. Seemingly similar to other fare of the day like *Take Her, She's Mine* and *I'll Take Sweden* – snickering comedies about a father's discomfort over the budding of his suddenly comely teen daughter – *Billie* doesn't boast a standard-issue comedy starlet like Sandra Dee or Tuesday Weld; instead it offers up short, ungainly, butch Patty Duke. Hoping in vain to cover this miscasting, the title tune insistently blares, "She looks like a Billie should look, wears her hair like a Billie should wear, walks like a Billie should, talks like a Billie should, on her a Billie looks good!"

(Erm... okay.)

Unhappy that (Warren) Berlinger treats her as "a girl first", Duke angrily vows to beat him at the Big Track Meet. She wins the day – and a date with him to (Jim) Backus' campaign gala. In a pink party dress, her hair teased to pass muster as a Dee do, Duke gushes, "Being a girl is so much fun, I've decided to give up track". Then, to let us know she'd only been flirting with feminism, she sings, "I am the girl that's a girl and I'm proud as I can be! Just to be glad I'm a girl is my greatest victory!" Duke's autobiography states Billie was shot in 15 days; it looks more like 15 minutes. Find this video, for a guaranteed hoot every 15 seconds.

On Feb. 7, 2011, Ashley posted:

I just watched this movie and I can't believe how it ended. I was so happy thinking that this girl was not only transgendered but also a feminist and was going to show all the chauvinistic pigs she knew what she was made of. Big disappointment. :(

DEAD AIR WEBSITE, by Daisy Deadhead, October 14, 2013

I saw *Billie* as a kid, and remembered it as being about a tomboy trying to femme it up for a boy she develops a crush on. And yes, it surely IS, but it now seems *far more insidious* and awful in its mid-60s har-har-har misogyny than I *ever* remembered. (I sometimes wonder what it did to me, mindlessly ingesting this kind of thing during my formative years. *Yighhhh!* Terrifying to contemplate.)

Billie is FAR WORSE than the nice girl/hell-raiser dichotomy we ate up on weekly installments of *The Patty Duke Show*. For example, one line intended to be funny, Billie/Patty whines, "I wish I was a boy!" and Jim Backus, her Dad, barks back, "Well, so do I, but you're not!" – something like that. Just awful. The movie is about Jim Backus (whom you know as the voice of Mr. Magoo or the redoubtable Thurston Howell the III) running for mayor of Anywhere, USA, and he has assured the town conservatives that females should *never* compete with males... and then the track team coach asks super-fast Billie (at left) to be on the team. (It is understood that this means the boys' team, since at that time, there *were* no girls' teams.) HORRORS! This might cost her Dad the election (!) and Jim Backus/Thurston Howell tries to make her quit the team.

It goes without saying that Billie falls in love with a boy on the team, who is not as fast as SHE is... and the feminist good news is, by the end of the movie, our young prince doesn't mind that Billie can beat him at sports. But it is *only* since she has properly feminized herself (*finally* all dolled up in high-school-dance drag, wearing a short dress and heels) and has also given him her HEART, that this is so. An interesting, and very lucidly-presented message about heterosexual romance TAMING the dangerous demon that is *women careening about* on sports teams and so forth: As long as they are f---able, cute and know their place, it's okay. Even if she is a *famous television star*!

There is actually a short blog on the movie, called *Billie's got the Beat*. It would appear this is ALSO a cult movie now. (shudders)

Long live Patty! We love you!

CYNTHIA BYRD TURNER – HEALTH ARTICLE, 2013

Is There a Rhythm to Life and Success? Did Patty Duke's Billie Have the Answer?

Finding your own rhythm of life can be an important key to finding success, no matter your definition of success.

Just what is rhythm? Rhythm, when applied to music, is the tempo or the beat of a song. When applied to life it is the tempo or the flow of life. Everyone has a rhythm. Some of us move through life swiftly and frenetically. Others take life a bit more languidly and 'go with the flow'. What is right for you?

When considering that being in sync with your rhythm of life is the key to success, I'm reminded of actor Patty Duke, starring as a teenager who won at track and field events by using a special trick: when she lined up at the starting blocks, she would 'listen' for her song or beat to play in her head.

You could see Patty catch the rhythm and come out of the blocks 'synced' with the beat of the music which became the beat of her success. She listened to that rhythm as she ran the track and won the race or jumped the highest hurdle, time and again. She was so successful, the coach of the boys' team asked her if this special rhythm technique was something she could teach others.

Remember, this was before iPods. The rhythm was truly in her head; a creation of her mind. Look at the athletes today who seem to have the rhythm, if the presence of iPods is any indication. Can you say Michael Phelps, Gold Medalists?

Can this be applied to the way you live your life? Do you have a rhythm for life, a rhythm for success? Have you found that inner song, the inner beat that buoys you along, conquering the discordant notes and pushing you past your competitors?

Finding your inner rhythm, finding your beat, if you will, can be a powerful tool for success. Even when life tosses in random discord that smooth rhythm is going to carry you along, just as it carried Patty Duke's character to the finish line.

Tapping into that rhythm is probably never easy and, unfortunately, probably not even recognized as a necessity by many. For Patty Duke's character, the goal was short term although if you watched this movie, there

Patty Duke as "Billie"

were lots of inferences to finding her rhythm off the track as well. For you, your rhythm will emerge as you uncover your strengths and act on them.

INTERNET DATABASE POSTS:

• Patty looks like a cute puppy-dog tomboy, and brings an intense energy to her role as Billie. After this film, she would never again appear so baby-faced and innocent. *(Sonja, May 8 2009)*

• Long Before the L word... Is 'tomboy' even used any more? In the nearly half-century since *Billie* was made, Americans have been exposed to masculine girls from Cher in *Silkwood* to Ellen Morgan (a.k.a. DeGeneres) to Patty Bouvier. In short, and citing in the immortal headline of Private Eye magazine, homosexuality has gone in from being the love that dare not speak its name to the love that won't shut up.

Billie could never, ever be made again in Hollywood. Any modern teen-angst movie about a tomboy would inevitably, in 2010, raise questions of homosexuality. Not that Billie is a Lesbian. Gee, gosh, and golly, no. There isn't even a suggestion of it. However – and accuse me of profiling, if you will, because I am – my gaydar was spinning like Brian Boitano the moment Duke sprinted onto the track field, looking for all the world like a pint-size peroxide Pete Rose.

Meanwhile, I couldn't help but wonder what teen-aged girls at the time – future Lesbians such as Christine Kehoe and Janis Ian and Suze Orman – thought when boyish Billie passionately admits "I wish I was a boy," only to have her father reply frankly, "So do I." It was a moving moment when Billie was just a tomboy to 15-year-old me; now that I view her as possibly a latent Lesbian, it was quite a powerful moment. *(Irie212, NYC, Oct. 28 2010)*

• Is Billie the first teen superheroine? Okay, we're not talking Hit-Girl or Kitty Pryde. But there's always been an unreal quality to Patty Duke's iconic tomboy Billie, as if she were a living cartoon, in everything from her appearance to an unmistakable 'super power' – The Beat, apparently an advanced psychic (or magical?) skill that endows her with superior physical strength, enabling Billie to 'beat' male opponents in every sport imaginable. Even when she teaches this remarkable skill to far better trained, super-athletic male students, she can still best them, probably because she's a pure source (in several ways). Indeed, Billie's distinctive Harding High track suit might as well be her official heroine 'costume' ('H' for Hoyden, maybe. It's Hoyden Girl!). More often than not she's running around in abbreviated shorty-shorts, showing off her sexy legs like most superheroines do without even thinking about it. All of which must be quite empowering to love of her life Mike Benson, who can quell this teen fury whenever he wants with a few well-meaning but chauvinistic words. Taking advantage of puppy love from someone who looks like a human puppy, he manages to convince our bright-eyed young Amazon to give up a) her passionate love for competition and besting males, and b) her unique God-given super power that no one seems able to match. And why? So she can wash his socks and cook his meals and eventually have his children. I always thought Hoyden Girl wouldn't put up with that arrangement for long. Billie should use The Beat to belt Benson right in the nose, put on the 'H' suit again, and show the local boys what for! *(Altara2, Jan. 18 2011)*

REACTIONS TO POSTED "BILLIE" TRAILER ON YOUTUBE:

• They should have made it a law that patty duke only be allowed to wear shorts lol my jaw hit the floor *(Cakimento)*

• Most look at this movie and compare Patty's (lesbian like) hair cut to the very Public lesbian Ellen Degeneres. I don't think because a woman has a short blond hair cut she is a lesbian. I have to admit it so cute Billie saying she wished she was a boy. LOL *(Jimmy82022000)*

• Everybody's favorite butch gal musical – what's not to like? *(HurricaneRhonda)*

• All she needed was the dot earrings and she would've been a full-fledged woman gym-teacher! *(FORESTJASPER)*

• This is where Psy got Gangnam from. Patty Duke style. *(Moorek1967)*

AMAZON.COM CUSTOMER REVIEWS:

• Can't believe I've written hundreds of reviews and not a word on *Billie*, one of the most original screen musicals of the 1960s. OK, maybe original isn't the right word.
  Patty Duke, well, what can I say. She was still running on her manic energy in 1965 and this was one of her very best roles. She's not as dumpy as other reviewers make her sound, although the dialogue in which the coach calls her "five feet two and a half inches of speed" is carefully contrived; surely she's not even five foot tall, she's tiny, and Susan Seaforth as her sexy older sister, home from a 'college back East' and pregnant, towers over her even in flats; it's there representing two different species in some Noah's Ark pageant of strange animals. But Patty looks great with blonde hair, and she's very appealing and, dare I say it, rather sexy, in the tight fitting athletic clothes teens wore in the old days I guess – now they look like dance leotards – Bob Fosse might have choreographed the big track meet in which humpy white boys in thigh hugging shorts carry triumphant, gender-variant Patty Duke high atop their heads, while the marching band plays an endless instrumental version of the title tune.
  Yes! It is strange that in a musical, there's only 4 songs, and two of them are exactly the same and filmed in exactly the same way, only their lyrics are different. Why? Was it some sort of Lars Von Trier experiment? There's a

sinister, Dogme 95 air to the staging of both "Lonely Little In-Between" and "Funny Little Butterflies". If there's a remake of *Billie*, I would put Björk in it right away, and Ben Gazzara could play the Jim Backus part, and it would be a fearsome condemnation of American politics, which it is already. *(Kevin Killian, October 3 2007)*

PATTY DUKE AS BILLIE YAHOO FAN GROUP

Selections from Conversation posts:

• In the movie, Billie's controversial 'answer' is to grow up in a hurry, put the tracksuit away (presumably forever) and embrace teen romance without looking back. Today, a 'Billie' would probably discover romance with her caring and patient boy (or girl) friend somewhere along the line, and then try to balance both her athletic world and her social/romantic life, without one abruptly cancelling out the other. That's what makes people nowadays diverse, interesting, and far more complicated than the endearing archetypes of the '50s and early '60s. *(tranzini101, March 15 2007)*

• (...recalling an interview with Patty Duke, where she said) "Only a year ago was I finally able to admit I can't sing and I have six albums to prove it!" To relieve Patty's pain, I brought up her other cult films, like *Billie*, in which she plays a Brandon Teena-like tomboy (an "in-between") who's force-feminized. "If they remade it today," she said, "she'd either come out of the closet or she'd disassociate from those who don't get her until they do." *(official_pattyduke, July 2007)*

• Dear Bill, Thanks so much for joining up and providing such interesting insights. That *Valley of the Dolls* reunion must have been a hoot! For the record, "Official Patty Duke" is Bill's fabulous Yahoo site (check it out and join ASAP), and he's been in the forefront of Patty Duke fandom (clubs, newsletters, etc.) for some time now.

As for *Billie*, what started out as an innocent family comedy in the spirit of *Gidget*, *Tammy* and Hayley Mills movies of the period, has now taken on a controversial new meaning. In an era where once-shunned alternative sexual lifestyles are not only accepted by mainstream culture, but celebrated and encouraged, 1965's *Billie* plays to many (including Ms. Duke herself) as an embarrassing, dated cop-out. Of course, at no time during the movie does Billie seem attracted to other girls, and the only thing that suggests that she's a latent lesbian is that she wears her hair short and excels in sports. The fact that she honestly enjoys her new boyfriend's embrace is dismissed as a dishonest 'token straight' moment; we all know that Billie's gay, filmmakers just couldn't come out (pardon the expression) and say it back in the mid-60s.

Frankly, I think there's a little 'gay pride' projection going on in this analysis/conclusion. On the surface at least, *Billie* was simply the old chestnut about a teen tomboy who comes of romantic age and gives up playing baseball (or whatever) for the joys of first love. Unless the statistics are lying, the overwhelming majority of young women in America do exactly the same thing. Some schoolgirls are indeed lesbians (it's part of the landscape), and a few actually become professional sports figures (why the hell not?). But most grow up, get married, and think back on their rough-and-tumble tomboy years with nostalgic fondness... even if many of these kids were "lonely little in-betweens" during their awkward, child-becomes-adult teenage phase.

Of course, current minds find it absurd that a movie with a central character like Billie could ONLY be about something so relatively trivial. But just how trivial is the film's true, central theme? Gay projections aside, *Billie* is really about an All-American teenage girl who defies the conventions of sexist '60s society by competing athletically with boys. As Billie herself points out, it's her legal as well as moral right to do so. While the adults huff and puff at the beginning of the story, they eventually come around to her intelligent, fair-minded way of thinking. At the very same time, Billie's experiencing her first crush on a boy she happens to like in a rather conventional, heterosexual way, and the two storylines soon dovetail. It's important to point out that our heroine clearly enjoys her impressive athletic endeavors, but at no point do we get the feeling that she's obsessed with pro-sports as an adult career... it's just something she likes to do as a precocious fifteen-year-old. When Billie finally gives up track, it's because a) she's successfully defied authority and proven her point, and b) she's lost interest in school sports (again, like the majority of girls facing their later teens) and would rather spend time smooching with good-looking guys than running them into the ground. Fair enough. Or maybe, after squabbling with so many 'adults', she's matured to the point where she prefers challenging males intellectually rather than physically. As far as recommending an adult career for Billie, I'd say she has the makings of an excellent lawyer, one that would defend the rights of the downtrodden, abused and manipulated individual to the bitter end.

My Devil's Advocate position: Movies, like art, are interpretative experiences, with the viewer ultimately seeing what he needs to see. Visually, Billie Carol does indeed come across as something of a gay icon. Given the repressive climate of the times, homosexuals clearly found comfort in any mainstream character that appeared kindred or sympathetic. Our track-running hoyden easily fit the bill, and her 'outsider angst' only reinforced it. Additionally, Patty Duke is an offbeat actress of rare depth (unlike, say, Sandra Dee), and her sophisticated line readings couldn't help but suggest that there was way more beneath the surface than met the eye. Ultimately, if gay viewers wanted to look upon Billie as a homosexual role model, they certainly had that right. We must never forget that these abused Americans were deprived of fundamental self-respect and societal inclusion back in the day, a shameful record by anyone's standards.

In my opinion, however, Billie as presented in the movie is an even greater feminist/lover of democracy than a more overt homosexual incarnation would be, because her issues are more broad-based. She refuses to be categorized, either by the conservative dummies that surround her, or left-wing progressives who would happily ignore who she truly is in order to satisfy their own political agenda. If Billie as a character represents anything, it's the unshakeable spirit of free choice. Conservatives think she's "crazy" for challenging "physically superior boys" on the sports field. Liberals think she's "copping out" because she ultimately loses interest in being a track star, puts on a dress and dates her boyfriend. Bottom line: as a gifted young woman with a mind and romantic inclinations of your own, the choice of future endeavors rests with you, Billie Carol. And from what I've seen and heard, you're smarter, fairer, and more of a free-thinking individual than any of your social/political critics.

So... what do YOU think about the great *Billie* controversy? C'mon, club members! Sound off! *(Tranzini101, July 3 2007)*

OFF TRACK: BILLIE AND GENDER LESSONS by Jamie Skerski, PhD

The 1965 family musical *Billie* is symptomatic of the gender dynamics of the era – representing the emerging politics of second wave feminism and the backlash against changing gender norms. Ahead of its time, *Billie* portrays a female protagonist fighting for a level playing field nearly a decade before the passage and implementation of Title IX, and a glimpse into a world dictated not by gender binaries, but by men and women as 'equals'. Widely seen as a film about tomboy angst, and despite the progressive potential of Patty Duke's tomboy character, Billie Carol, the film ultimately reinforces the relinquishment of tomboy agency and empowerment in service of heterosexual femininity.

Some viewers read a lesbian subtext in the narrative, but this ultimately collapses: Billie is not unsure of her sexuality, she has simply not yet seen herself as an object of male desire. She is, perhaps unfortunately, more naïve than actually questioning her identity. When her track teammate, Mike, is caught staring at her body while she's dancing in the backyard, she doesn't recognize his desire. Later, when Mike actually confesses his affection while they're dancing and reveals he "likes" her, Billie misinterprets his intentions and confirms their friendship, exclaiming they are such good friends that he's "almost like a sister."

Despite being portrayed as one of the more progressive characters in the film, Mike doesn't get the hint. He brushes off Billie's lack of reciprocal feelings and proceeds to hold her hand on the way home from that dance. Interestingly, Mike's unrequited advances become the catalyst for the rest of the film – Billie has now recognized herself in the male gaze. She returns home from that hand-holding moment to tell her mother that she "felt strange... like a girl." Cue the music. Billie retreats once again to her teenage bedroom to perform the song, *Funny Little Butterflies*, singing: *I must be growing up... I felt butterflies... I'm still a little scared – it happened way too fast.*

While the lyrics once again problematically mention a lack of consent (*it happened way too fast*), there is no turning back for Billie after she experiences those butterflies, as is almost always the case for tomboys in popular narratives. The next day at track practice, Billie loses her interest in the competition and allows Mike to win the race. But, as they spend more time together and Mike asks Billie to quit the track team to protect his own masculine identity, we see a glimpse of the old feminist-minded Billie, as she storms off to proclaim "that all men stink" and sets out to win the upcoming track meet.

In the end, Billie does indeed win the track meet, outrunning all of the men and even her love interest, Mike. She is carried off on the shoulders of her teammates and, for a moment, it seems *Billie* is a film about female excellence and empowerment. Mike even admits that Billie isn't "his equal, but his better." But, it doesn't end there. The film concludes with Billie, donned in a sleeveless pink dress and make-up, attending her father's mayoral victory party as Mike's date. As the night rolls on, she reveals a secret to her father, as they dance. She whispers in his ear, "Being a girl is so much fun... I've decided to give up track." Nobody suggests otherwise.

What is perhaps most troubling in this particular narrative is the contradictory messages about choice and agency. On one hand, Billie 'chooses' her transformation. It is, after all, her decision to give up track. However, Billie also *accepts this change as inevitable and natural,* just as the songs suggest, as a part of 'growing up'. Thus, *Billie* is less a story about a triumphant tomboy, and more a tale about the inevitability of accepting normative gender roles. Billie's final song proclaims the film's loudest message: *Just to be glad I'm a girl, is my biggest victory… that's what I was meant to be.*

The Beat Goes On

Son of Ginger

BILLIE'S REAL DAD, WRITER RONALD ALEXANDER, DIED OF CANCER ON APRIL 24, 1995 at age 78. He not only lived long enough to watch his endearingly subversive creation flourish in a variety of venues, but, in 1980, he penned a sequel: *Time and Ginger*.

    This sassy-but-occasionally-serious continuation is superior in just about every way, with the author honing in on rich gender-related observations mixed seamlessly with high-spirited, semi-cartoonish, wonderfully eccentric humor. Shockingly, but perhaps inevitably, the always-headstrong Ginger/Billie winds up marrying her old lunkhead arch-nemesis, Eddie Davis. Tables turned, it's their own kids who are driving them crazy with dicey social antics (fearless daughter Winnie is a 'so what?' unwed mother long before Juno). Then there's a friend of their oddball teenage son Tink, named… Billie, offering Alexander an opportunity to explore "lonely little in-between" social issues and the gay question more openly than ever before.

Revealing herself to be half-Irish and therefore partially insane ("Any race that believes that little people live under mushrooms has to be touched with madness"), forty-two-year-old Ginger is a hoot of a housewife, keeping befuddled Eddie on his ideological toes while humoring long-suffering visiting Dad Howard Carol, who, true to form, has some of the play's funniest lines (and seems to have trouble seeing, a Jim Backus-Mr. Magoo in-joke, perhaps).

As usual, Ginger's pithy views of male and female behavior take center-stage, and have become even less inhibited with the seasoning of adulthood, proving such a thing is possible. The interesting case of her grandmother, discussed with Eddie, is a good example. At age 89, the woman drives, plays tennis, skis, and wants a divorce after seventy-four years of marriage. "Women have a greater sense of inevitability, they *bend* with time…" Mrs. Ginger Davis nonchalantly explains. "Men generally break because they try to stand up to it. That's why they become impotent… and eventually senile." Husband Eddie, older and far wiser when it comes to sparring with his childhood spitfire, seems to take this observation philosophically. "Since your father seems so happy," he tells her like a defeated soldier, "I can hardly wait for the second stage."

Time and Ginger played well enough in off-Broadway incarnations, receiving positive reviews more often than not, but never made it to the big time like its iconic predecessor. Available in print from online sources, this is a fun read, especially if you imagine the adult, world-aware Patty Duke speaking all these outrageous lines.

Ginger in the 21st Century

Although out of favor for a number of years, the word 'tomboy' roared back to popularity in the first decade of the 21st Century, the way the word 'girl' was

In March and April of 2011, the Unitarian Universalist Congregation of Atlanta presented an incarnation of Time Out for Ginger *set in the 1950s, like Ronald Alexander's original.*

Other local stage versions update the material to present-day America, where 'girl power' has finally come into its own as a social phenomenon.

When the original pilot to the unsold Time Out for Ginger *TV series resurfaced circa 2008, it was of interest to fans and historians who were curious about the content. Being in the public domain, it also wound up in the hands of a cultish comedy group known as the Kids on the Street, who put it up on YouTube with an added commentary track by C. Glen Williams. As is usually the case in send-ups like this, the obligatory quips aren't as humorous as the film's accidental shortcomings. But to be fair, the Kids hit the jackpot with this hilarious poster they created to match their video; it captures Candy Moore's hyper-manic take on Ginger perfectly.*

forgiven and re-championed in the late 1990s. Briefly considered obsolete once young American women were encouraged to become more active in high-profile sports, 'tomboy' soon became synonymous with unbridled, intellectually-astute, rebellious female anger, generally directed against conservative or traditionally male social limitations. Things got incrementally more serious when Middle Eastern countries began banning tomboys and their defiant lifestyle, deeming boyish behavior in girls an affront to traditional Muslim beliefs (and inspiring waves of protests from pissed-off toms). Adding to the new century furor, German scientists gamely announced possible methods to 'cure' tomboys before they are born with some fancy gene tampering, pleasing parents who want less sporty and boisterous, more feminine and frilly daughters. Amazingly enough, the Billies of tomorrow may be fighting not only for their civil rights, but for their very existence.

With cute-but-punkish role models like Avril Lavigne, Ellen Page, Sarah Silverman, Amanda Bynes, Keira Knightley and others selling tomboyism with redefined, f--- you millennial flavoring, the grandmommy of all hoyden parables, *Time Out for Ginger* seemed a logical candidate for updating. Naturally, the play's original 'sell-out' ending had to be re-worked for modern audiences and the rough-and-tumble girl power material could now be played with more kick-ass gusto. It's hardly surprising that this semi-intense leading role continues to attract the interest of free thinking actresses… and now of all races, with Mexican and Asian Gingers adding yet another layer of cultural interest to Alexander's likeable scenario.

The Beat is Back: Billie Animated

Rumors of a live-action *Billie* prime-time series, possibly to replace the aging *PDS* circa '66 and starring Miss Duke in vibrant color, have persisted over the years, based on interesting but inconclusive 'evidence' provided by eager fans. A second theory suggests a Duke-less TV sitcom incarnation, with a different cute teenager stepping into those running shorts. A Saturday morning cartoon version for ABC has also been mentioned as a dim-memory possibility. Significantly, when Patty Duke herself was recently asked if she recalled any of these *Billie* spinoffs, she couldn't honestly say she did. Perhaps just as significantly, she added that some of these projects could have been developed without her knowledge, possibly pitched to ABC by others, such as Peter Lawford's minions. The sheer logic of evolving such a TV-friendly property into its next creative incarnation has helped to lend a degree of credibility to this mostly fan-based speculation.

Whatever may or may not have happened in the past, Beat-blessed Billie seems a logical candidate for re-booting, having come into her own rather dramatically in the feminist-dominated, ass-kicking 21st Century. As altara2 points out in his IMDb post, The Beat, coupled with her 'H' for Hoyden uniform and physical look, makes Billie something of a teenage superheroine. While this take is a far cry from the kind of serious *Billie* Ms. Duke herself would prefer for a remake – a sweet bit of honesty that could make an absolutely wonderful film – a colorful animated series, with the style and wit of, say, *Kim Possible*, would have its own attendant charms. It could also say some important things about boy-girl relations that would serve as primers for more serious thought, while entertaining the heck out of kids with spirited action-adventure in the meantime.

Once again guided by logic, we coyly present a modern take on the Billie character, a rebellious heroine as inherently cool as those PowerPuff sprites, the aforementioned Ms. Possible, and the most audacious new-age tomboy of all, Hit-Girl. The designs and sketches here are by **Rock Baker**, an appealing combo of retro-cool and modern anime. Now, as in 1966, obnoxious jock Eddie Davis serves quite nicely as a tricky rival/comedy relief foil, bested by Billie at every turn. Wile E. Coyote and the Road Runner for a jaded generation, perhaps? Or, if one prefers, Bluto vs. the female equivalent of Popeye, her energizing Beat a reasonable substitute for the sailorman's spinach. Now, for maximum satisfaction as you peruse the new Billie, punch up a little Miley Cyrus, kick back, and consider the possibilities!

Meant to match the retro-fun tone of these drawings, but with a little edge, is an excerpt from an extended caption as published in the public blog *Billie's Got the Beat* (http://billiebeat.blogspot.com):

"MAY THE BEST ATHLETE WIN!"

Two contenders for Harding's most anticipated Triathlon event stand side-by-side for a quick interview. And already the fur is starting to fly.

"I'm not a girl, I'm an Equal," insists sixteen-year-old Billie Carol, ready for high-speed action against formidable male competitors in her tracksuit, form-fitting shorts and sneaks. As a matter of fact, many experts consider this bright-eyed young female not only equal to the male jocks in her orbit, but better. *Way* better. Tapping into an inner source of rhythmic power that dramatically amplifies her physical prowess, mop-topped Billie can outplay and outfight any guy at anything. Track, football, pole-vaulting, kickboxing... you name it!

On the other hand, "That silly tomboy is always underfoot, getting in the way of serious athletes, like myself," proclaims local sports star Eddie Davis, Billie's most persistent and least tolerant rival. "She needs to grow up in a hurry, maybe put on a dress once in a while to remind herself she's a girl. Instead, she drives all the jocks around here crazy with her annoying antics."

Billie just rolls her eyes. "Well as a rule, I try not to say anything negative about a fellow athlete," she explains patiently. "But the truth is, I get a real rush when I run blowhard bullies like Davis here into the ground. It's like, what's the matter, Fast Eddie... your legs aren't long enough?"

"Y'know one of these days I'm gonna lose my cool and give this pushy brat the spanking she deserves!"

"Just try it, musclehead!" Billie snaps back.

"Grow up, runt!"

Unfazed and energized, Billie sticks out her tongue and wiggles her fingers in defiant response. Then she dashes away from the interview site, down the schoolyard track… an infuriated Eddie Davis hot on her sneakered heels.

With the 'Beat' as her inner ally, an overjoyed Billie races far, far ahead… The blonde dynamo's gotten such a distance away from Eddie that she actually stops and turns to look back at him, confidently placing fists-on-hips and shaking her head. Apparently this sort of thing happens all the time. "Hey, Mr. Macho! What's keeping you?" Billie gleefully shouts to her far-off, pathetically pumping opponent. Then she energetically gives Davis la finger and continues her supersonic run.

Ahh, The Beat! Billie's very own built-in weapon against boy braggarts, jealous jocks, and old school thinkers who believe girls should behave more demurely. It's that driving rock 'n' roll rhythm in her head that gets this young woman racing like a rocket. She smokes the competition not only in running contests, but by performing heavy-duty gymnastic feats and even physical combat moves. "Bring it on!" laughs the tracksuited teen wonder of Harding High, always ready to square off with overconfident, underhanded bully blowhards like Eddie Davis. "And don't forget to bring plenty of bandages!"

With The Beat on Billie's side, there's no way she can lose!

THE END?!

End Game:
Some Final Thoughts

WE'VE HEARD IT ALL NOW, THE THEORIES AND CONCLUSIONS, FROM JUST about every side. So, was this little social experiment in pop cultural interpretation a success?

For what it's worth, debaters Casey Bond and I found ourselves honestly caught up all over again with this movie's subtle-yet-potent subtext, the '60s bubblegum flavors bringing us right back to our early Beatles, 007 teenhood. As has been said endlessly, all of us Baby Boomers grew up with the wonderful, irreplaceable Patty Duke.

And, speaking of Anna, in our initial interview we promised readers a direct answer to this study's subtitled question: Role Model or Sell Out? Here's what the Oscar-winning actress finally had to say...

"Role Model. For her day, Billie was very courageous. She stood up, not only to her peers and her parents, but to all the authority figures in her world who were trying to say, women weren't meant for certain things. She knew better. She caved at the end because of first love, but she was only 15. I wish I was as gutsy at her age!"

Thanks so much, Anna. In the final analysis, maybe we're all sell-outs in some ways, role model champions in others. If *Billie* is a significant film beyond its gaudy 'mod musical' camp value, it's because it has found a way to ask some serious and provocative questions without ever abandoning warmth and hope. Movies like this rarely win Oscars, but they sneak up on Boomers years later, their buried insights suddenly becoming more apparent as time strips away 20th Century denial.

Final performance evaluation? Pay attention, gentlemen. We can all learn a thing or two from the girl with The Beat!

Additional Reading...

HERE ARE SELECTED BOOKS (AND ONE VIDEO) RELATING TO OUR SUBJECT. Note that most of these studies were made in the first two decades of the 21st Century, as American feminism became mainstream, dovetailing with popular 'girl power' media bombardment.

Aapola, S., Gonick, M., & Harris, A. *Young Femininity: Girlhood, Power and Social Change*, Palgrave Macmillan New York (2005).

Abate, Michelle A. *Tomboys: A Literary and Cultural History*, Temple University Press (2008).

Akert, Julie; Christian McEwen. *Tomboys! Feisty Girls and Spirited Women*, Akeret Films (28 minute video; 2004).

Andrea. "Girls Will Be Tomboys," *The Feminist Hivemind* (2013).

Bailey, J. Michael; Bechtold, Kathleen T.; Berenbaum, Sheri A. "Who Are Tomboys and Why Should We Study Them?", *Archives of Sexual Behavior*, Vol. 31, No 4 (August 2002).

Burn, Shawn Megan, A. Katherine O'Neil, and Shirley Nederend. "Childhood Tomboyism and Adult Androgyny," *Sex Roles 34* (1996): 419–428. Web. 10 (2010).

Butler, J. *Gender Trouble: Feminism and the Subversion of Identity*, Routledge, New York (1990).

Carr, C. L. "Tomboy resistance and conformity: Agency in social psychological gender theory", *Gender and Society*, 12(5), 528-553 (1998).

Driscoll, C. *Girls: Feminine Adolescence in Popular Culture & Cultural Theory*, Columbia University Press, New York (2002).

Duke, Patty; Turan, Kenneth. *Call Me Anna: The Biography of Patty Duke*, Bantam Books (2011).

Halberstam, Judith. *Female Masculinity*, Duke University Press, Durham (1998).

Halim, May Ling; Dalmut, Elizabeth; Greulich, Faith K.; Ahlqvist, Shean; Lurye, Leah E.; Ruble, Diane N. "The Role of Athletics in the Self-Esteem of Tomboys," *Child Development Research, Volume 2011*, Article ID 830245 (2011). Also: "The Potential Benefits and Risks of Identifying as a Tomboy: A Social Identity Perspective," *Research Gate* (2012).

Additional Reading...

Harris, Adrienne. "Gender as a Soft Assembly: Tomboys' Stories", *Studies in Gender and Sexuality* (2003). Also: *All About the Girl: Culture, Power and Identity*, Routledge, London. (2004a). Also: Harris, A. *Future Girl: Young Women in the Twentieth-First Century.* Routledge, London (2004b).

Hatch, Kristen. "Little Butches: Tomboys in Hollywood Film," *Meditated Girlhoods/Meditated Youth Series.* Peter Lang Publishing (2011).

Hugenkamp, K. D., & Livingston, M. M. "Tomboys, masculine characteristics and self-ratings of confidence in career success", *Psychological Reports*, 90, 743-749 (2002).

Mitchell, Claudia; Reid-Walsh, Jacqueline. *Girl Culture: An Encyclopedia.*

Morgan, Betsy Levonian. *A Three Generational Study of Tomboy Behavior, Sexy Roles*, Volume 39, Plenum Publishing/Springer Science+Business Media. University of Wisconsin (1998).

Paechter, C., & Clark, S. "Who are tomboys and how do we recognize them?", *Women's Studies International Forum*, 30, 342-354 (2007).

Quimby, Karin. "The Story of Jo: Literary Tomboys, Little Women, and the Sexual-Textural Politics of Narrative Desire," *GLQ: A Journal of Lesbian and Gay Studies*, Volume 10, Number 1 (2003).

Reay, D. "'Spice Girls', 'Nice Girls', 'Girlies' and 'Tomboys': Gender discourses, girls' cultures and femininities in the primary classroom," *Gender and Education*, 13(2), 153-66 (2001).

Renold, E. "'They won't let us play... unless you're going out with one of them': Girls, boys and Butler's 'heterosexual matrix' in the primary years," *British Journal of Sociology of Education*, 27(4): 489-509 (2006). Also: "Beyond masculinity?: Re-theorising contemporary tomboyism in the schizoid space of innocent/(hetero) sexualised femininities," *International Journal of Girlhood Studies*, 1(2).

Robinson, K., & Davies, C. "Tomboys and Sissy Girls: young girls' negotiations of femininity and masculinity," *International Journal of Equity and Innovation in Early Childhood*, 5(7), 17-31 (2007). Also: "'She's kickin' ass, that's what she's doing': Deconstructing childhood 'innocence' in media representations," *Australian Feminist Studies*, 23(57), 343-358 (2008a).

Schmich, Mary. "How We Separate Girls from Tomboys," *Chicago Tribune News* (1994).

Skersky, Jamie. "Tomboy Chic: Re-fashioning Gender Rebellion," *Journal of Lesbian Studies*, Vol. 15, issue 4 (2011). Also: *Taming the Tomboy: Gender Lessons in Post Title IX America* (book manuscript in progress).

Thorne, B. *Gender play: Girls and boys in school.* New Brunswick N.J: Rutgers University Press (1993).

Walkerdine, V. *Daddy's girl: Young girls and popular culture.* Basingstoke: Macmillan (1997). Also: *Growing up girl: Psychosocial explorations of gender and class.* London: Palgrave (2001).

Zevy, Lee. "Lesbian Tomboys and "Evolutionary Butch." *Journal of Lesbian Studies 8*: 143–158. Routledge Taylor and Francis Group. (2004).

... and Viewing

There are countless tomboy-themed movies, but the "competition with men" angle, at the heart of *Billie*, was given center-stage in a number of high-profile productions. A few of these films were discussed in this book, a few weren't. Here's a sampling:

ANNIE GET YOUR GUN (MGM, 1950) offered up quintessential tomboy Betty Hutton as the famed sharpshooter who, like our very own Billie, forsakes career fulfillment for love of a hunk (Howard Keel, surely hunkier than Warren Berlinger).

PAT AND MIKE (MGM, 1952). Kate Hepburn made a career out of playing tomboys, but this romp about a female golf phenom ups the ante by practically surrounding her with sexist romantic leads. Hepburn's own regressive fiancée is inevitably dispensed with, while grouchy/shady sports manager Tracy has his attitude adjusted after Kate clobbers two male harassers to protect him (something Billie only *threatens* to do when her chauvinistic Mike appears to need help).

CALAMITY JANE (Warner Brothers, 1953). Now it's a bullwhip-cracking Doris Day who needs feminizing, with rootin'-tootin', face-scrunching Jane even more exaggerated than Annie. Clearly a re-working of *AGYG*, *Jane* squeezes its shapely star into the equivalent of a frontier catsuit, although none of Calamity's cowboy pals see past her boisterous bravado. That includes love interest Bill Hickok, with loaned-from-MGM Howard Keel once again recruited to tame a tomboy shrew.

TOMBOY (Crown International, 1985). Essentially an '80s teen exploitation flick, *Tomboy* nevertheless showcases the rivalry between a female auto racer and her hunky boyfriend, another high-speed driver. Not only does feisty and super-sexy Betsy Russell whip her opponent on the track, she clobbers him with a pretty mean slam to the stomach (ughh!!) during an impromptu boxing match. Reflecting its post Title 9, feminist-empowered era, *Tomboy* ends with the titular heroine not having to choose between a sports career or romance: she can have it all, and does.

About the Authors

GARY GERANI is a professional screenwriter (Stan Winston's *Pumpkinhead*), graphic novelist (*Bram Stoker's Death Ship*, *Dinosaurs Attack!*), children's product developer (hundreds of products for Topps), film and TV historian (1977's *Fantastic Television*), award-winning art director (for renderings by Drew Struzan, Jack Davis, Joe Smith, etc.), photo editor, designer, and publisher (the Fantastic Press trade paperback series). Gerani is currently writing/editing new *Star Wars* trading card sets for Topps, while developing books that explore his earlier SW creations. A native East Coaster, he grew up in Bensonhurst, Brooklyn, but currently resides in Sherman Oaks, California. He often travels back to the old neighborhood for both business and pleasure.

CASEY BOND is also a native of Brooklyn NY who now resides and works as an educational counselor on Long Island by day... and performs as a professional doumbek player (Middle Eastern hand drum) in NYC by night! She's proud to perform with belly dance bands such as "Carmine & Friends" and "Scott Wilson & Efendi" and her world music trio "The Scheherezade Project". She teaches percussion at The Harem Belly Dance Studio in Baldwin, New York, is the artistic director of her student percussion ensemble

"Raq Steady" and is the featured drummer on the CD "Live at JeBon" (www.cdbaby.com/scottwilson3). Although her son Peter and daughter Colette are full-grown, this book will remind them to use the catchphrase she taught them to explain her quirkiness when they were very small: "Mother is eccentric!"

www.ingramcontent.com/pod-product-compliance
Lightning Source LLC
Chambersburg PA
CBHW071442150426
43191CB00008B/1208